A KEY

WAVERLEY NOVELS

a

OPINIONS OF THE PRESS

(Alphabetically arranged)

~~~~~~~~~~

'The entire essence of the stories.'—*Bedfordshire Mercury.*

'A valuable and exceedingly handy little work.'—*Court Journal.*

'We heartily commend this very happy idea.'—*Ecclesiastical Gazette.*

'Another useful work by Mr Grey.'—*Edinburgh Courant.*

'An admirable idea carried out with great literary skill.'--*Glasgow Herald.*

'The plot of each novel is carefully condensed in as few words as possible.'—*Graphic.*

'Very skilfully and attractively epitomised.'—*Hampshire Telegraph.*

'A marvel of compactness.'—*Harper's Magazine.*

'Written in a very attractive manner.'—*Jersey Express.*

'Admirably compiled.'—*Manchester Courier.*

'The plots are clearly set forth.'—*New York Critic.*

'The principal scenes are vividly sketched.'—*North Wales Guardian.*

'Will be welcomed by a large class of readers.'—*Ontario Chronicle.*

'Will be read with interest and advantage.'—*Oxford Chronicle.*

'Gives a lucid outline of the plots.'—*Oxford and Cambridge Undergraduates' Journal.*

'Very successfully condensed.'—*People's Journal, Dundee.*

'A very careful summary.'—*St Andrews Gazette.*

'Gives a very pithy outline of each tale.'—*School Newspaper.*

'Fits into the wards of each story in the smoothest fashion.'—*Sunday Times.*

'Capitally done.'—*Tablet.*

'Unlocks several historical obscurities.'—*Wakefield Herald.*

'A veritable *multum in parvo*.'—*Worcestershire Chronicle.*

NEW EDITION

A KEY TO THE
WAVERLEY NOVELS

IN CHRONOLOGICAL SEQUENCE

WITH INDEX OF THE PRINCIPAL CHARACTERS

BY

HENRY GREY

F.R.B.S., F.Z.S., F.I.Inst.

AUTHOR OF

'AN EPITOME OF THE BIBLE' 'THE CLASSICS FOR THE MILLION'
'A BIRD'S-EYE VIEW OF ENGLISH LITERATURE'
'TROWEL, CHISEL, AND BRUSH' 'A POCKET ENCYCLOPÆDIA'
'THE PLOTS OF OLD ENGLISH PLAYS'
'RESTING WITHOUT RUSTING' 'ZOO NOTES'
'SCIENCE NOTES' 'SIXTY-FIVE YEARS' REMINISCENCES'
ETC. ETC.

HASKELL HOUSE PUBLISHERS Ltd.

Publishers of Scarce Scholarly Books

NEW YORK. N. Y. 10012

1973

HASKELL HOUSE PUBLISHERS Ltd.

Publishers of Scarce Scholarly Books

280 LAFAYETTE STREET

NEW YORK. N. Y. 10012

Library of Congress Cataloging in Publication Data

Grey, Henry.
  A key to the Waverley novels.

   1. Scott, Sir Walter, bart., 1771-1832. Waverley
novels. 2. Scott, Sir Walter, bart., 1771-1832--
Dictionaries, indexes, etc. 3. Scott, Sir Walter,
bart., 1771-1832--Characters. I. Title.
PR5341.G8 1973   823'.7   73-6987
ISBN 0-8383-1699-9

Printed in the United States of America

PREFACE

THESE brief sketches of the Historical Novels by Sir Walter Scott,—whom Lord Meadowbank eulogised as 'The mighty magician, who has rolled back the current of time, and conjured up before our living senses the men and manners of days which have long since passed away,'—are offered to the public with the hope that, to those who have read the Tales (which fill ten thousand closely printed pages, and extend over a period of more than seven hundred years), they may serve as a memento of the principal scenes and characters ; and to those who have not, as an appetising foretaste of the intellectual feast in store for them.

H. G.

CONTENTS

Date of the Story.		PAGE
1098.	COUNT ROBERT OF PARIS	1
1187.	THE BETROTHED	5
1191.	THE TALISMAN	9
1194.	IVANHOE	14
1306.	CASTLE DANGEROUS	18
1402.	THE FAIR MAID OF PERTH	22
1468.	QUENTIN DURWARD	27
1474.	ANNE OF GEIERSTEIN	31
1550.	THE MONASTERY	35
1567.	THE ABBOT	39
1575.	KENILWORTH	43
1600.	DEATH OF THE LAIRD'S JOCK	48
1604.	THE FORTUNES OF NIGEL	50
1645.	A LEGEND OF MONTROSE	54
1652.	WOODSTOCK	58
1678.	PEVERIL OF THE PEAK	62
1679.	OLD MORTALITY	67
1695.	THE BRIDE OF LAMMERMOOR	71
1700.	THE PIRATE	75
1702.	MY AUNT MARGARET'S MIRROR	80

Date of the Story.		PAGE
1706.	THE BLACK DWARF	82
1715.	ROB ROY	86
1736.	THE HEART OF MID-LOTHIAN	90
1745.	WAVERLEY	94
1763.	REDGAUNTLET	98
1765.	GUY MANNERING	103
1775.	THE HIGHLAND WIDOW	107
1780.	THE SURGEON'S DAUGHTER	109
1782.	THE TAPESTRIED CHAMBER	113
1795.	THE TWO DROVERS	115
1795.	THE ANTIQUARY	117
1812.	ST RONAN'S WELL	121

INDEX OF THE PRINCIPAL CHARACTERS . . . 125

A KEY TO THE
WAVERLEY NOVELS

COUNT ROBERT OF PARIS

Principal Characters

ALEXIUS COMNENUS, *Greek Emperor of Constantinople.*
THE EMPRESS IRENE, *his wife.*
PRINCESS ANNA, *their daughter.*
NICEPHORUS BRENNIUS, *her husband.*
ASTARTE,
VIOLANTE, } *her attendants.*
ACHILLES TATIUS, *officer of the Imperial Varangian Guard.*
HEREWARD, *an Anglo-Saxon, his subaltern.*
STEPHANOS CASTOR, *a wrestler.*
LYSIMACHUS, *a designer.*
HARPAX, *centurion of the city guard.*
SEBASTES, *a recruit in the corps.*
NICANOR, *commander-in-chief of the Greek army.*
ZOSIMUS, *Greek patriarch.*

MICHAEL AGELASTES, *an old sage.*
GODFREY DE BOUILLON,
PETER THE HERMIT,
COUNT BALDWIN,
COUNT DE VERMANDOIS,
BOHEMOND OF ANTIOCH,
PRINCE TANCRED OF OTRANTO,
RAYMOND, COUNT OF TOULOUSE, } *leaders of the first Crusade.*
COUNT ROBERT OF PARIS,
BRENHILDA, *Countess of Paris.*
TOXARTIS, *a Scythian chieftain.*
AGATHA, *afterwards* BERTHA, *Hereward's betrothed.*
DIOGENES, *a negro slave.*
ZEDEKIAS URSEL, *a rival for the throne.*
DOUBAN, *a slave skilled in medicine.*
SYLVAN, *an ourang-outang.*

Greek citizens, courtiers, military officers, seamen, soldiers, priests and slaves. Army of Crusaders.

Period, 1098. *Localities: Constantinople and Scutari.*

EIGHT hundred years ago Constantinople—then as now unrivalled as regards the beauty of its situation on the confines of Europe and Asia—

A

was threatened by barbarians from the east, and by the Franks from the west. Unable to rely on his Greek subjects to repel their incursions, the emperor was obliged to maintain a body-guard of Varangians, or mercenaries from other nations, of whom the citizens and native soldiers were very jealous. One of these, Hereward, had just been attacked by Sebastes, when Tatius intervened and led him to the palace. Here he was introduced to the imperial family, surrounded by their attendants ; and the Princess Anna was reading a roll of history she had written, when her husband entered to announce the approach of the armies composing the first Crusade. Convinced that he was powerless to prevent their advance, the emperor offered them hospitality on their way ; and, the leaders having agreed to acknowledge his sovereignty, the various hosts marched in procession before his assembled army.

As Comnenus, however, moved forward to receive the homage of Count Bohemond, his vacant throne was insolently occupied by Count Robert of Paris, who was with difficulty compelled to vacate it, and make his submission. The defiant knight, accompanied by Brenhilda, afterwards met the sage Agelastes, who related the story of an enchanted princess, and decoyed them to his hermitage overlooking the Bosphorus. Here they were introduced to the empress and her daughter, who, attended by Brennius, came to visit the sage, and were invited to return with them to the palace to be presented to the emperor. At the State banquet which followed, the guests, including Sir

Bohemond, were pledged by their royal host, and urged to accept the golden cups they had used. On waking next morning, Count Robert found himself in a dungeon with a tiger, and that Ursel was confined in an adjoining one. Presently an ourang-outang descended through a trap-door, and afterwards Sebastes, both of whom the count had overpowered, when Hereward made his appearance, and undertook to release his Norman adversary.

A treasonable conference was meanwhile taking place between Tatius and Agelastes, who had failed in endeavouring to tamper with the Anglo-Saxon; and the countess had been unwillingly transported by Diogenes to a garden-house for a secret interview with Brennius, whom she challenged to knightly combat in the hearing of her husband. Having hidden the count, Hereward encountered his sweetheart Bertha, who had followed Brenhilda as her attendant, and then obtained an audience of the imperial family, who were discussing recent events, including a plot in which Brennius was concerned for seizing the throne, and received permission to communicate with the Duke de Bouillon. Bertha volunteered to be his messenger, and, at an interview with the council of Crusaders at Scutari, she induced them to promise that fifty knights, each with ten followers, should attend the combat to support their champion.

Having made his confession to the Patriarch, while Agelastes was killed by Sylvan as he argued with Brenhilda respecting the existence of the devil, the emperor led his daughter to the cell in which Ursel was confined, with the intention of making him her husband, instead of Brennius. She had, however, been persuaded by her mother to intercede for the traitor, and Ursel was merely placed under the care of Douban to be restored to health after his long imprisonment. Alexius had decided that Brennius should fight the Count of Paris, instead of the countess, and all the preparations for the combat had been made, when the ships conveying the Crusaders hove in sight; and, after defeating the Greek fleet, they landed in sight of the lists. Brennius, in the meantime, was pardoned, and, in answer to shouts of discontent from the assembled crowd, Ursel was led forth to announce his restoration to liberty and the imperial favour, and the conspiracy was crushed. Hereward then appeared to do battle with Count Robert, and, saved from the knight's axe by Bertha, he joined the Crusaders, obtaining on his return the hand of his betrothed, and, ultimately, a grant of land from William Rufus, adjacent to the New Forest in Hampshire, where he had screened her when a girl from the tusk of a wild boar.

THE BETROTHED

Principal Characters

GWENWYN, *Prince of Powys-land.*
BRENGWAN, *his wife.*
FATHER EINION, *his chaplain.*
CADWALLON, *his principal bard.*
JORWORTH AP JEVAN, *a messenger.*
BALDWIN, *Archbishop of Canterbury.*
SIR RAYMOND BERENGER, *of Garde Doloureuse.*
His daughter, EVELINE.
His sister, A BENEDICTINE ABBESS.
FATHER ALDROVAND, *his chaplain.*
DENNIS MOROLT, *his squire.*
REINOLD, *his butler.*
RAOUL GILLIAN, *his huntsman.*
DAME GILLIAN, *his wife.*
SIR HUGO DE LACY, *Constable of Chester.*

DAMIAN LACY, *his nephew.*
RANALD LACY, *their kinsman.*
PHILIP GUARINE, *Sir Hugo's squire.*
AMELOT, *Damian Lacy's page.*
RALPH GENVIL, *his banner-bearer.*
WILLIAM FLAMMOCK, *a Flemish weaver.*
His daughter, ROSE, *Eveline's waiting-maid.*
ERMINGARDE, *the Lady of Baldringham.*
BERWINE, *her housekeeper.*
HUNDWOLF, *her steward.*
SIR GUY MONTHERMER, *in command of the King's troops.*
THE EARL OF GLOUCESTER.
KING HENRY II.
PRINCE RICHARD, } *his sons.*
PRINCE JOHN,

Norman cavaliers, Welsh borderers, soldiers, camp followers, minstrels, pedlars, mendicants, outlaws, peasants; general assembly.

Period, 1187. *Locality: Wales.*

THE archbishop, as he travelled and preached among them, had exhorted the Britons, and the Anglo-Normans who were settled on the borders of the Welsh principalities, to lay aside their feuds, and join in the third Crusade. Accordingly, the Prince of Powys-land and the Knight of Garde

5

Doloureuse had accepted each other's hospitality, and Gwenwyn, at the suggestion of his chaplain, had arranged to divorce his wife, in order that he might marry Sir Raymond's daughter. In reply to his proposal, however, a messenger brought a letter stating that she was promised to the Constable of Chester, which being taken by the Welsh as an affront, the call to war was sung by the bards, the Norman castle was attacked, and its owner slain in a combat with his would-be son-in-law. Nerved by the presence of Eveline on the battlements, and supplied with food by a ruse of her father's vassal the Flemish weaver, the garrison, assisted by the military predilections of their chaplain, held out until Damian Lacy arrived with a large force, when the brave but unarmoured Britons were repulsed, and their prince was killed. Having granted an interview to her deliverer, Eveline was escorted by her suitor the Constable, and a numerous retinue, to her aunt's nunnery. On her way thither she passed a night at the house of a Saxon kinswoman, the Lady of Baldringham, where she occupied a haunted chamber, and saw the ghost of an ancestor's wife, who foretold that she would be—

> ' Widowed wife, and married maid,
> Betrothed, betrayer, and betrayed.'

During her visit to the abbess she was formally espoused to Sir Hugo ; but the archbishop having the next day commanded him to proceed to Palestine for three years, he offered to annul their engagement. Eveline, contrary to her aunt's advice, promised to await his return; and it was arranged that she should reside in her castle, with Rose and Dame Gillian as her attendants, and Damian as her guardian. Wearied with her monotonous life during this seclusion, she was induced one day to join in a hawking expedition unaccompanied by her usual escort, and was seized by rebels secretly instigated by Ranald Lacy. In attempting to rescue her Damian was severely wounded, and she insisted on nursing him in the castle, while Amelot led his men-at-arms in pursuit of the outlaws, whose disaffection had reached the king's ears, with a rumour that Damian was their captain. Sir Guy Monthermer was, accordingly, sent to demand admittance to Garde Douloureuse, where he was reported to be concealed; and when Eveline ordered the portcullis to be dropped against him, a herald proclaimed her, and all who aided and abetted her, as traitors.

The constable and his squire, who were supposed to be dead, returned from Syria, disguised as palmers, just as the royal troops, headed by Prince Richard, had occupied the castle, Eveline at the same time being sent to a convent, and Damian consigned to a dungeon. Having learnt the ill news from old Raoul and his wife, Sir Hugo made his way towards King Henry's camp, near which, surrounded by an assembly of spectators, Ranald Lacy, who by false representations had obtained a grant of Eveline's forfeited lands, and assumed his kinsman's dress and title, was about to present a royal charter of immunities to a procession of the Flemish settlers. Cadwallon, the

Welsh bard, had, however, attached himself to
Sir Hugo as a Breton minstrel, in order that he
might avenge the death of Gwenwyn ; and mis-
taking Ranald for the returned constable, suddenly
sprang behind him as he leant forward in his
saddle, and stabbed him in the back. Sir Hugo
now made himself known, and was welcomed by
the king, the assassin was executed, and, convinced that his betrothed's love had been given
to Damian, the old Crusader resigned her to him,
and consoled himself by taking part in the sub-
jugation of Ireland.

THE TALISMAN

Principal Characters

SIR KENNETH OF THE COUCH-
ANT LEOPARD, *Prince Royal
of Scotland.*
STRAUCHAN, *his squire.*
ILDERIM SHEERKOHF, *a Sara-
cen Emir.*
THEODORIC OF ENGADDI, *a
Christian hermit.*
KING RICHARD I., *one of the
Council of the third Crusade.*
QUEEN BERENGARIA, *his wife.*
LADY CALISTA OF MOUNT-
FAUCON, *her attendant.*
LADY EDITH PLANTAGENET,
Richard's kinswoman.
NECBATANUS, *the Queen's dwarf.*
GUENEVRA, *his lady-love.*

EL HAKIM, *a physician; after-
wards* SULTAN SALADIN.
THE ARCHBISHOP OF
TYRE,
THE GRAND-MASTER OF
THE TEMPLARS,
THE MARQUIS CONRADE
OF MONTSERRAT,
THE ARCHDUKE LEO-
POLD OF AUSTRIA,
KING PHILIP AUGUSTUS
OF FRANCE,
EARL WALLENRODE, *an Hun-
garian warrior.*
A MARABOUT, *or Turkish
fanatic.*
BLONDEL, *King Richard's min-
strel.*

other members of the Council.

SIR THOMAS DE MULTON,
SIR THOMAS DE VAUX OF
GILSLAND,
} *in attendance on the King.*

*Choir of boys and maidens; knights and soldiers of the Christian
and Mohammedan armies.*

Period, 1191. *Locality: Syria.*

DURING a truce between the Christian armies
taking part in the third Crusade, and the infidel
forces under Sultan Saladin, Sir Kenneth, on his
way to Syria, encountered a Saracen Emir, whom he
unhorsed, and they then rode together, discoursing

on love and necromancy, towards the cave of the hermit, who was in correspondence with the pope, and to whom the knight was charged to communicate secret information. Having provided the travellers with refreshment, the anchorite, as soon as the Saracen slept, conducted his companion to a chapel, where he witnessed a procession, and was recognised by the Lady Edith, to whom he had devoted his heart and sword. He was then startled by the sudden appearance of the dwarfs, and, having reached his couch again, watched the hermit scourging himself until he fell asleep.

About the same time Richard Cœur de Lion had succumbed to an attack of fever, and as he lay in his gorgeous tent at Ascalon, the Scot arrived accompanied by a Moorish physician, who had cured his squire, and who offered to restore the king to health. After a long consultation, and eliciting from Sir Kenneth his visit to the chapel, the physician was admitted to the royal presence; and, having swallowed a draught which he prepared from a silken bag or talisman, Richard sank back on his cushions. While he slept Conrade of Montserrat secretly avowed to the wily grand-master his ambition to be King of Jerusalem; and, with the object of injuring Richard's reputation, incited Leopold of Austria to plant his banner by the side of that of England in the centre of the camp. When the king woke the fever had left him, and Conrade entered to announce what the archduke had done. Springing from his couch, Richard rushed to the spot

and defiantly tore down and trampled on the
Teuton pennon. Philip of France at length persuaded him to refer the matter to the council, and
Sir Kenneth was charged to watch the English
standard until daybreak, with a favourite hound
as his only companion. Soon after midnight,
however, Necbatanus approached him with Lady
Edith's ring, as a token that his attendance was
required to decide a wager she had with the
queen; and during his absence from his post
the banner was carried off, and his dog severely
wounded. Overcome with shame and grief, he
was accosted by the physician, who dressed the
animal's wound, and, having entrusted Sir Kenneth with Saladin's desire to marry the Lady
Edith, proposed that he should seek the Saracen
ruler's protection against the wrath of Richard.
The valiant Scot, however, resolved to confront
the king and reveal the Sultan's purpose; but it
availed him not, and he was sentenced to death,
in spite of the intercessions of the queen and
his lady-love; when the hermit, and then the
physician, arrived, and Richard having yielded to
their entreaties, Sir Kenneth was simply forbidden
to appear before him again.

Having, by a bold speech, revived the drooping
hopes of his brother Crusaders, and reproved the
queen and his kinswoman for tampering with the
Scot, Richard received him, disguised as a Nubian
slave, as a present from Saladin, with whom he
had been induced to spend several days. Shortly
afterwards, as the king was reposing in his pavilion,
the slave saved his life from the dagger of an

assassin secretly employed by the grand-master, and intimated that he could discover the purloiner of the standard. A procession of the Christian armies and their leaders had already been arranged in token of amity to Richard; and as they marched past him, seated on horseback, with the slave holding the hound among his attendants, the dog suddenly sprang at the Marquis Conrade, who was thus convicted of having injured the animal, and betrayed his guilt by exclaiming, ' I never touched the banner.' Not being permitted to fight the Teuton himself, the king undertook to provide a champion, and Saladin to make all needful preparations for the combat. Accompanied by Berengaria and Lady Edith, Richard was met by the Saracen with a brilliant retinue, and discovered, in the person of his entertainer, the physician who had cured his fever, and saved Sir Kenneth, whom he found prepared to do battle for him on the morrow, with the hermit as his confessor. The encounter took place soon after sunrise, in the presence of the assembled hosts, and Conrade, who was wounded and unhorsed, was tended by the Sultan in the grand-master's tent, while the victorious knight was unarmed by the royal ladies, and made known by Richard as the Prince Royal of Scotland. At noon the Sultan welcomed his guests to a banquet, but, as the grand-master was raising a goblet to his lips, Necbatanus uttered the words *accipe hoc*, and Saladin decapitated the templar with his sabre; on which the dwarf explained that, hidden behind a curtain, he had seen him stab his accomplice the Marquis of Montserrat, obviously to prevent him from revealing their infamous plots, while he answered his appeal for mercy in the words he had repeated. The next day the young prince was married to Lady Edith, and presented by the Sultan with his talisman, the Crusade was abandoned, and Richard, on his way homewards, was imprisoned by the Austrians in the Tyrol.

IVANHOE

Principal Characters

CEDRIC THE SAXON, *of Rother-wood Grange.*
WILFRED OF IVANHOE, *his disinherited son.*
THE LADY ROWENA, *his ward, beloved by Ivanhoe.*
GURTH, *his swineherd.*
WAMBA, *his jester.*
SIR PHILIP DE MALVOISIN, *a neighbour.*
THE PRIOR OF AYMER, *Abbot of Jourvaulx.*
SIR BRIAN DE BOIS GILBERT, *a Norman knight-templar.*
ISAAC OF YORK, *a Jew money-lender.*
His daughter, REBECCA.
PRINCE JOHN, *brother of Richard I.*
ATHELSTANE, *a Saxon knight, Ivanhoe's rival.*

LOCKSLEY, *alias* ROBIN HOOD, *an outlaw.*
REGINALD FRONT DE BŒUF,
RICHARD DE MALVOISIN,
HUGH DE GRANTMESNEL,
RALPH DE VIPONT,
MAURICE DE BRACY, } *Norman knights-templar.*
FRIAR TUCK, *of Copmanhurst.*
DAME ULRICA, *of Torquilstone.*
KING RICHARD I., *returned from the third Crusade.*
LUCAS DE BEAUMANOIR, *grandmaster of the Templars.*
CONRADE DE MALVOISIN, *his attendant knight.*
HIGG, *a Saxon peasant.*

Servants, knights, and squires at a tournament, Saxon outlaws.

Period, 1194. *Localities: Yorkshire and Leicestershire.*

THE Anglo-Saxons had not yet overcome their antipathy to their Norman conquerors ; and when the prior and Sir Brian, with a pilgrim as their guide, sought the hospitality of Rotherwood on their way to a tournament, they were received with haughty dignity. At the evening meal Lady Rowena was inquiring the latest news from

Palestine, whither her lover had gone, and Isaac
had craved shelter from the stormy night, when
Cedric elicited that Ivanhoe had gained as much
renown as any of King Richard's Norman knights,
and Sir Brian offered to fight him; on which the
pilgrim exclaimed, 'I'll be his surety,' and Lady
Rowena gaged her honour on his behalf. The
Jew was conducted by Wamba to his cell, and
during the night, with Gurth's assistance, he and
the pilgrim started for Ashby, near which town
rich and poor were assembling to witness a
passage of arms between several knights-templar,
led by Sir Brian, in the presence of Prince John.
The champions entered the lists attended by pur-
suivants and heralds, and, after several encounters,
the conquerors challenged any other knights
present to meet them, when one in sable armour,
with the word 'disinherited' on his shield, defied
Sir Brian. At the second charge the Norman
was unhorsed; and, having with equal prowess
disposed of four other antagonists, the unknown
victor exercised his privilege by naming Lady
Rowena as the queen of the day.

Isaac had provided him with a horse and
armour, and Gurth was now sent to pay him
for them with the money with which the van-
quished knights had redeemed theirs. In the
next day's sports Ivanhoe was recognised by his
father and Lady Rowena, and, having received
a wound, was taken charge of by the Jew and
his daughter, the chief honours being awarded
to Locksley and another knight in black armour.
The latter, however, disappeared, and made his

way to the hermitage of Friar Tuck, a disguised bandit. Meanwhile, Cedric and his ward, as well as Isaac, Rebecca and Ivanhoe, had been seized in the adjacent forest by Front de Bœuf and his followers, dressed as outlaws, and carried to the castle of Torquilstone, where De Bracy and Sir Brian demanded the hands of their female captives, and the Jew was threatened with torture unless he agreed to pay a heavy ransom. Rebecca was about to throw herself from a window, when the sound of a bugle announced the arrival of Locksley and his followers, accompanied by the black knight. Having escaped from Sir Brian, the Jewess found Ivanhoe in an adjoining room, and with him watched the attack on the castle. After a desperate struggle the defenders were overpowered, the prisoners released, and the stronghold set on fire. Having thanked their preservers, Cedric and Rowena returned home, leaving Wamba to attend the black knight; and the Jew went in search of his daughter, who had been carried off by Sir Brian, bearing a letter to him from Prior Aylmer, who had also been confined in the castle, intimating that he had better give her up.

The following morning Prince John, who hoped to usurp the throne, received intelligence that his brother was in England; and, the prior's letter having fallen into the hands of the grand-master, preparations were made for the trial of Rebecca as a witch. The peasant Higg was unwillingly brought forward to prove that she had cured him of a sore disease, and other witnesses falsely

deposed to acts of sorcery which she had prac-
tised.   She, however, claimed trial by combat,
and was allowed to send a messenger to her
father.   The same evening the black knight was
attacked in the forest by several armed men, and,
just as he was unhorsed, Locksley with a band
of yeomen came to his rescue.   Ivanhoe also
rode up, and having done homage to him as
King Richard, announced Rebecca's need of a
champion.

The bell was tolling at the castle occupied by
the knights-templar, the fagots were ready, and
the lists prepared for her doom or rescue, the
grand-master was seated on his throne, and Sir
Brian had whispered her to escape with him, when
a mounted knight was seen advancing.   A herald
demanded his name, and he answered 'Wilfred of
Ivanhoe'; the trumpets sounded the charge, and
although the Saxon's horse fell, the templar rolled
from his saddle, and on his helmet being raised
he was dead.   The silence of the spectators was
broken by the arrival of the king, at whose command Conrade de Malvoison was arrested for high
treason, and the grand-master, having threatened
to appeal to Rome, withdrew with his knights and
followers; Rebecca at the same time leading her
father away lest Richard should incarcerate him
in order to obtain a loan, and fearful also of
betraying her secret love for her deliverer.   The
nuptials of Ivanhoe and Rowena quickly followed ;
and, having presented the bride with a casket of
jewels of immense value, the Jew and his daughter
quitted England to take up their abode at Granada.

B

CASTLE DANGEROUS

Principal Characters

BERTRAM, *an English minstrel.*
AUGUSTINE, *his supposed son;*
afterwards LADY AUGUSTA
of Berkely.
TOM DICKSON OF HAZELWOOD,
a vassal of the Douglas estate.
His son, CHARLES.
SIR JOHN DE WALTON, *Governor of Castle Douglas.*
SIR AYMER DE VALENCE, *Deputy Governor.*
FABIAN HARBOTHEL, *his squire.*
GILBERT GREENLEAF, *an old archer.*
ABBOT JEROME, *of St Bride's convent.*

SISTER URSULA; *afterwards*
LADY MARGARET DE HAUTVILLE.
SIR MALCOLM FLEMING, *her lover.*
MICHAEL TURNBULL, *a border forester.*
LAZARUS POWHEID, *sexton of Douglas Kirk.*
THE KNIGHT OF THE TOMBS;
afterwards SIR JAMES DOUGLAS.
THE BISHOP OF GLASGOW.
THE EARL OF PEMBROKE.

English soldiers, squires and pages, inhabitants of Douglas,
Scottish knights and fighting men.

Period, 1306. *Localities: Ayrshire and Lanarkshire.*

DURING the struggle for the Scottish crown between Edward I. and Robert Bruce, the stronghold of his adherent Sir James Douglas, known as Castle Dangerous, had been taken by the English, and Lady Augusta had promised her hand and fortune to Sir John de Walton, on condition that he held it for a year and a day. Anxious to curtail this period, she determined to make her way thither, accompanied by her father's minstrel, disguised as his son, and they were

18

within three miles of their destination, when
fatigue compelled them to seek shelter at Dickson's farm. Two English archers, who were
quartered there, insisted that the youth should
be left at the neighbouring convent of St Bride's,
until Bertram satisfied Sir John as to the object
of their journey, and this arrangement was ap-
proved of by Sir Aymer, who arrived to visit the
outpost. As they proceeded together towards the
castle, the minstrel entertained the young knight
with some curious legends respecting it, including
the supernatural preservation of an ancient lay
relating to the house of Douglas, and the future
fate of the British kingdom generally. De Valance
would at once have passed the stranger into the
stronghold as a visitor; but Gilbert Greenleaf detained him in the guard room until the arrival of
the governor, who, in the hearing of Fabian, expressed his disapproval of his deputy's imprud-
ence, and thus the seeds of disagreement were
sown between them.

Sir John, however, wished to be indulgent to his
young officers, and accordingly arranged a hunting party, in which the Scottish vassals in the
neighbourhood were invited to join; but, at the
mid-day repast, Turnbull behaved so rudely to
the governor that he ordered him to be secured,
when he suddenly plunged into a ravine and disappeared. The young knight too' fresh offence
at being ordered to withdraw the archers from the
sport to reinforce the garrison, and appealed to
his uncle, the Earl of Pembroke, who, instead of
taking his part, wrote him a sharp reproof. He

then opposed the governor's wish that the minstrel
should terminate his visit, which induced Sir John
to threaten Bertram with torture unless he instantly
revealed his purpose in coming to the castle. The
minstrel declined to do so without his son's permission ; and, the Abbot having pleaded for delay
on account of the boy's delicate health, Sir Aymer
was ordered to meet a detachment at an outpost,
and then to bring him to the castle to be examined.
As he passed through the town he encountered a
mounted warrior in full armour, whom neither the
inhabitants nor his followers would admit having
seen. The old sexton, however, declared that the
spirits of the deceased knights of Douglas could
not rest in their graves while the English were at
enmity with their descendants. On reaching the
convent, De Valence roused Father Jerome, and
insisted that the youth should at once accompany
him. He was, however, allowed to return to his
bed till daybreak, and upon the door of his room
being then forced open, it was empty. During the
night, Sister Ursula, who had hidden in the room,
elicited Lady Augusta's secret, which she had
already guessed, and, having narrated the circumstances under which she had entered the convent
without taking the vows, they escaped through a
concealed postern and found a guide with horses
waiting for them. A scroll which his lady-love
had left behind her explained matters to Sir John,
who, in his despair, was comforted by the sym-
pathy of his lieutenant ; and the faithful minstrel,
having been admitted to their confidence, steps
were at once taken to track the fugitives.

Having reached a thicket, Lady Margaret disappeared to join her friends, and Lady Augusta was escorted, first by the celebrated Douglas, and then by Turnbull, to a spot where they met Sir John, to whom the forester delivered a message with which he refused to comply, and mortally wounded the man when he attempted to lead the lady away. But Sir James was at hand, and the two knights fought until summoned by the church bells to Palm Sunday service, at which the old bishop officiated in the presence of an excited assemblage of armed English and Scotch warriors eager to attack each other. Bertram met Lady Augusta in the churchyard, and was arranging for her safety, when De Walton and The Douglas renewed their combat, and an encounter also took place between De Valence and Sir Malcolm Fleming. The life of the latter was saved by the intercession of Lady Margaret, and Sir John surrendered his sword and governorship on the arrival of a messenger with the intelligence that an English force, commanded by the Earl of Pembroke, which was advancing to prevent an anticipated attack on the castle, had been utterly defeated by Bruce and his followers. He and his troops, however, were allowed to retire with their arms, Sir James having chivalrously transferred his claim upon her lover to the Lady Berkely, who, in return for his courtesy, decorated the brave Scotchman with a chain of brilliants which had been won in battle by her ancestor.

THE FAIR MAID OF PERTH

Principal Characters

OLD SIMON, *a glover in the Couvrefeu, Perth.*
His daughter, CATHARINE.
His apprentice, CONACHAR ; *afterwards* EACHIN M'IAN, *Chief of the Clan Quhele.*
HENRY GOW, *an armourer and burgess of Perth.*
FATHER FRANCIS, *a Dominican monk.*
FATHER CLEMENT, *a Carthusian monk.*
OLIVER PROUDFUTE, *a bonnet-maker.*
BAILIE CRAIGDALLIE.
HENBANE DWINING, *an apothecary.*
SIR PATRICK CHARTERIS, *of Kinfauns, Provost of Perth.*
KIT HENSHAW, *his servant.*
THE DEVIL'S DICK, *of Hellgaith, a follower of The Douglas.*
PRIOR ANSLEM, *of St Dominic's Convent.*

KING ROBERT III.
DAVID, DUKE OF ROTHSAY, *his son.*
THE DUKE OF ALBANY, *the king's brother.*
THE EARL OF MARCH.
LOUISE, *a minstrel from Provence.*
ARCHIBALD, EARL OF DOUGLAS.
SIR JOHN RAMORNY, *the prince's master of the horse.*
EVIOT, *his page.*
ANTHONY BONTHRON, *an assassin.*
SIR LOUIS LUNDEN, *town-clerk of Perth.*
LINDSEY, EARL OF CRAWFORD.
THE EARL OF ERROL, *Lord High Constable.*
TORQUIL OF THE OAK, *Eachin's foster father.*
MACGILLIE CHATTANACH, *Chief of the Clan Chattan.*

Midnight revellers, neighbours, council of citizens, men-at-arms, Highlanders, morrice-dancers, funeral procession on Loch Tay, pages, servants, rival clansmen, inhabitants of Perth.

Period, 1402. *Locality : Perthshire.*

THE armourer had excited the jealousy of Conachar by spending the evening with the glover and his daughter, and was returning to their house at dawn, that he, might be the first person she saw on St Valentine's morning, when he encountered a party of courtiers in the act of placing a ladder against her window. Having cut off the hand of one, and seized another, who, however, managed to escape, he left the neighbours to pursue the rest, and was saluted by Catharine as her lover. The citizens waited on the provost, who, having heard their grievance, issued a challenge of defiance to the offenders.

Meanwhile the king, who occupied apartments in the convent, had confessed to the prior, and was consulting with his brother, when the Earl of March arrived to intimate his withdrawal to the English Border, followed into the courtyard by Louise, and afterwards by the Duke of Rothsay, whose dalliance with the maiden was interrupted by the Earl of Douglas ordering his followers to seize and scourge her. Henry Gow, however, was at hand, and the prince, having committed her to his protection, attended his father's council, at which it was determined that the hostile Clans Chattan and Quhele should be invited to settle their feud by a combat between an equal number of their bravest men in the royal presence, and a commission was issued for the suppression of heresy. The old monarch, having learnt that his son was one of those who had attempted to force their way into the glover's house, insisted that he should dismiss his master of the horse, who encouraged all his follies ; and while Catharine, who had listened to the Lollard teaching of Father Clement, was being urged by him to favour the secret suit of the prince, her other lover, Conachar, who had rejoined his clan, appeared to carry off her counsellor from arrest as an apostate reformer.

The armourer had maimed Sir John Ramorny, whose desire for revenge being encouraged by the apothecary, Bonthron undertook to waylay and murder him. On Shrovetide evening old Simon was visited by a party of morrice-dancers, headed by Proudfute, who lingered behind to confirm a rumour that Henry Gow had been seen escorting a merry maiden to his house, and then proceeded thither to apologise for having divulged the secret. On his way home in the armourer's coat and cap, as a protection against other revellers, he received a blow from behind and fell dead on the spot. About the same time Sir John was roused from the effects of a narcotic by the arrival of the prince, who made light of his sufferings, and whom he horrified by suggesting that he should cause the death of his uncle, and seize his father's throne.

The fate of the bonnet-maker, whose body was at first mistaken for that of the armourer, excited general commotion in the city; while Catharine, on hearing the news, rushed to her lover's house and was folded in his arms. Her father then accompanied him to the town council, where he was chosen as the widow's champion, and the provost repaired to the king's presence to demand a full inquiry. At a council held the following day, trial by ordeal of bier-right, or by combat, was ordered; and suspicion having fallen on Ramorny's household, each of his servants was required to pass before the corpse, in the belief that the wounds would bleed afresh as the culprit approached. Bonthron, however, chose the alternative of combat, and, having been struck down by Gow, was led away to be hanged. But Dwining had arranged that he should be suspended so that he could breathe, and during the night he and Eviot cut him down and carried him off.

Catharine had learnt that she and her father were both suspected by the commission; and the provost having offered to place her under the care of The Douglas's daughter, the deserted wife of the prince, the old glover sought the protection of his former apprentice, who was now the chieftain of his clan. Having returned from his father's funeral, Conachar pleaded for the hand of Catharine, without which he felt he should disgrace himself in the approaching combat with the Clan Chattan. Simon, however, reminded him that she was betrothed to the armourer, and his foster father promised to screen him in the conflict. At the instigation of his uncle, the prince had been committed to the custody of the Earl of Errol; but, with the duke's connivance, he was enticed by Ramorny and the apothecary to escape to the castle of Falkland, and, with the help of Bonthron, starved to death there. Catharine and Louise, however, discovered his fate, and communicated with The Douglas, who overpowered the garrison, and hung the murderers.

The meeting of the hostile champions had been arranged with great pomp, and Henry Gow, having consented to supply Eachin with a suit of armour, volunteered to take the place of one of the Clan

Chattan who failed to appear, A terrible conflict ensued, during which Torquil and his eight sons all fell defending their chief, who at last fled from the battle-ground unwounded and dishonoured. On hearing of Rothsay's death, Robert III. resigned his sceptre to his wily and ambitious brother, and died broken-hearted when his younger son James was captured by the English king. Albany transferred the regency to his son; but, nineteen years afterwards, the rightful heir returned, and the usurper expiated his own and his father's guilt on the scaffold. The warrants against Simon and his daughter, and Father Clement, were cancelled by the intervention of the Earl of Douglas, and the Church was conciliated with Dwining's ill-gotten wealth. Conachar either became a hermit, or was spirited away by the fairies; and Scotland boasts of many distinguished descendants from Henry Gow and his spouse the Fair Maid of Perth

QUENTIN DURWARD

Principal Characters

QUENTIN DURWARD, *a Scotch cadet.*

LUDOVIC LESLEY, LE BALAFRE, *his maternal uncle.*

MAITRE PIERRE, *a merchant; afterwards* KING LOUIS XI.

TRISTAN L'HERMITE, *his provost-marshal.*

DAME PERRETTE, *hostess of ' The Fleur de Lys.'*

JACQUELINE, *her servant; afterwards* ISABELLE, COUNTESS OF CROYE.

LADY HAMELINE, *her aunt.*

LORD CRAWFORD, *commander of Scottish archers.*

COUNT DE DUNOIS, *grand huntsman.*

LOUIS, DUKE OF ORLEANS.

CARDINAL JOHN OF BELUE.

THE BISHOP OF AUXERRE.

OLIVER LE DAIN, *the court barber.*

PRINCESS BEAUJEAU, PRINCESS JOAN, *the king's daughters.*

COUNT PHILIP CRÉVECŒUR OF BURGUNDY.

THE COUNTESS, *his wife.*

TOISON D'OR, *his herald.*

WILLIAM DE LA MARCK, *a Flemish outlaw.*

CARL EBERSON, *his son.*

HAYRADDIN MANGRABIN, *a Bohemian.*

ZAMET, *his brother.*

MARTHON, *a gipsy woman.*

LOUIS OF BOURBON, *Bishop of Liège.*

PAVILLON, *a currier and syndic.*

His daughter, GERTRUDE.

PETERKIN GIESLAER, *his deputy.*

NIKKEL BLOK, *a butcher.*

DUKE CHARLES OF BURGUNDY.

LE GLORIEUX, *his jester.*

Scottish archers, peasants, gipsies, soldiers, citizens, guards, abbess, nuns, courtiers, etc.

Period, 1468. *Localities : France and Flanders.*

THE age of feudalism and chivalry was passing away, and the King of France was inciting the wealthy citizens of Flanders against his own rebellious vassal the Duke of Burgundy. Quentin

27

Durward had come to Tours, where his uncle was one of the Scottish body guard maintained by Louis XI., to seek military service, and was invited by the king, disguised as a merchant, to breakfast at the inn, and supplied by him with money. Having narrowly escaped being hung by the provost-marshal for cutting down Zamet, whom he found suspended to a tree, he was enlisted by Lord Crawford, and learned the history of Jacqueline. In the presence-chamber he was recognised by Louis, and the royal party were preparing for a hunting excursion, when the Count of Crévecœur arrived with a peremptory demand for the instant surrender of the duke's ward, the Countess of Croye, who had fled from Burgundy with her aunt to escape a forced marriage; and proclaimed that his master renounced his allegiance to the crown of France. In the chase which followed Durward saved the king's life from a boar, for which service Louis, after consulting with his barber, entrusted him with the duty of conducting the Countess and Lady Hameline, ostensibly to the protection of the Bishop of Liège, but really that they might fall into the hands of William de la Marck. After proceeding some distance they were overtaken by Dunois and the Duke of Orleans, who would have seized the countess, but were prevented by Lord Crawford, who arrived in pursuit and made prisoners of them. Then Hayraddin came riding after them, and under his guidance they journeyed for nearly a week, when Quentin discovered that the Bohemian was in league with De la Marck.

He accordingly altered their route, and they reached the bishop's castle in safety.

A few days afterwards, however, it was assaulted by the citizens, and Hayraddin having effected Lady Hameline's escape with Marthon, Quentin rushed back to save the countess, and, at Gieslaer's suggestion, Pavillon passed them as his daughter and her sweetheart into the great hall where the outlaw, who was known as the Boar of Ardennes, was feasting with the rioters. The bishop, who was also governor of the city, was then dragged in, and, having denounced his captor, was murdered by a stroke of Nikkel Blok's cleaver. There was a shout for vengeance, but De la Marck summoned his soldiers, upon which Quentin held a dirk at the throat of his son Carl, and exhorted the citizens to return to their homes. With the syndic's help Lady Isabella and her protector reached Charleroi, where she was placed in a convent, while he carried the news to the Duke of Burgundy, at whose court Louis, with a small retinue, was a guest. Charles, in a furious rage, accused the king of being privy to the sacrilege, and caused him to be treated as a prisoner.

At a council the following day he was charged with abetting rebellion among the vassals of Burgundy, and the countess was brought as a witness against him. She admitted her fault, and Quentin Durward was being questioned respecting his escort of her, when a herald arrived with a demand from De la Marck to be acknowledged as Prince-Bishop of Liège, and for the release of his ally the King of France. Louis replied that he intended

to gibbet the murderer, and the messenger, who
was discovered to be Hayraddin, was sentenced to
death, the quarrel between the duke and the king
being at the same time adjusted, on the understanding that the Duke of Orleans should marry
Lady Isabelle. Crévecœur, however, interceded for
her, and it was arranged that whoever should bring
the head of the Boar of Ardennes might claim her
hand. Quentin, who had learnt his plans from the
Bohemian, advanced with the allied troops of
France and Burgundy against his stronghold, and
a desperate battle ensued. At length the young
Scot was in the act of closing with De la Marck,
when Pavillon's daughter implored his protection
from a French soldier; and, while placing her in
safety, his uncle La Balafré fought the ruffian,
and carried his head to the royal presence. Lord
Crawford declared him to be of gentle birth, but
the old soldier having resigned his pretensions to
his nephew, King Louis vouched for Quentin's
services and prudence, and the duke being satisfied
as to his descent, remarked that it only remained
to inquire what were the fair lady's sentiments
towards the young emigrant in search of honour-
able adventure, and who, by his sense, firmness
and gallantry, thus became the fortunate possessor
of wealth, rank and beauty.

ANNE OF GEIERSTEIN

Principal Characters

JOHN PHILIPSON, *an English merchant; afterwards* EARL OF OXFORD.

ARTHUR DE VERE, *his son.*

ANTONIO, *their young Swiss guide.*

ARNOLD BIEDERMAN, *a magistrate of Unterwalden.*

RUDIGER,
ERNEST, }*his sons.*
SIGISMUND,

ANNE OF GEIERSTEIN, *his niece.*

ANNETTE VEILCHEN, *her attendant.*

RUDOLPH OF DONNERSHUGEL, *a Bernese.*

COUNT ALBERT OF GEIERSTEIN, *Anne's father.*

ITAL SCHRECHWALD, *his steward.*

CHARLES THE BOLD, DUKE OF BURGUNDY.

COUNT ARCHIBALD VON HAGENBACH, *his steward.*

NICHOLAS BONSTETEEN,
MELCHIOR STURMTHAL, }*Swiss deputies to the duke.*
ADAM ZIMMERMAN,

DANNISCHEMEND, *a Persian sorcerer.*

His daughter, HERMIONE.

JAN MENGS, *landlord of the 'Golden Fleece' in Rhenish Prussia.*

KNIGHTS AND BURGHERS OF THE VEHMIQUE TRIBUNAL.

MARGARET OF ANJOU, *widow of* KING HENRY VI.

KING RENE, *of Provence, her father.*

FERRAND DE VAUDEMOND, *Duke of Lorraine, his grandson.*

COUNT CAMPO BASSO, *commander of Italian mercenaries.*

Swiss youths and mountaineers, executioner, citizens and soldiers, guests at inn, army at Dijon, troubadours at Provence, Burgundian nobles and troops, Swiss patriots.

Period, 1474. *Localities : Switzerland, Germany and France.*

As the merchant and his son were travelling towards Basle they were overtaken by a storm, and found themselves at the edge of a precipice caused by a recent earthquake. Arthur was making his

way towards a tower indicated by Antonio, when
he was rescued from imminent danger by Anne,
who conducted him to her uncle's mountain home,
whither his father had been brought in safety by
Biederman and his sons. During their evening
games Rudolph, who had joined in them, became
jealous of the young Englishman's skill with the
bow, and challenged him ; but they were overheard by Anne, and the duel was interrupted.
The travellers were invited to continue their journey
in company with a deputation of Switzers, com-
missioned to remonstrate with Charles the Bold
respecting the exactions of Hagenbach ; and the
magistrates of Basle having declined to let them
enter the city, they took shelter in the ruins of a
castle. During his share in the night watches,
Arthur fancied that he saw an apparition of Anne,
and was encouraged in his belief by Rudolph, who
narrated her family history, which implied that her
ancestors had dealings with supernatural beings.
Hoping to prevent a conflict on his account between
the Swiss and the duke's steward, the merchant
arranged that he and his son should precede them ;
but on reaching the Burgundian citadel they were
imprisoned by the governor in separate dungeons.
Arthur, however, was released by Anne with the
assistance of a priest, and his father by Biederman,
a body of Swiss youths having entered the town
and incited the citizens to execute Hagenbach,
just as he was intending to slaughter the deputation, whom he had treacherously admitted. A
valuable necklace which had been taken from the
merchant was restored to him by Sigismund, and

the deputies having decided to persist in seeking
an interview with the duke, the Englishman undertook to represent their cause favourably to him.

On their way to Charles's headquarters father
and son were overtaken by Anne disguised as a
lady of rank, and, acting on her whispered advice
to Arthur, they continued their journey by different
roads. The elder fell in with a mysterious priest
who provided him with a guide to the 'Golden
Fleece,' where he was lowered from his bedroom
to appear before a meeting of the Vehmique or
holy tribunal, and warned against speaking of their
secret powers. The younger was met and conducted by Annette to a castle, where he spent the
evening with his lady-love, and travelled with her
the next day to rejoin his father at Strassburg.
In the cathedral there they met Margaret of Anjou,
who recognised Philipson as the Earl of Oxford,
a faithful adherent of the house of Lancaster, and
planned with him an appeal to the duke for aid
against the Yorkists. On reaching Charles's camp
the earl was welcomed as an old companion in
arms, and obtained a promise of the help he sought,
on condition that Provence was ceded to Burgundy.
Arthur was despatched to Aix to urge Margaret
to persuade her father accordingly, while the earl
accompanied his host to an interview with his
burghers and the Swiss deputies.

King René's preference for the society of troubadours and frivolous amusements had driven his
daughter to take refuge in a convent. On hearing from Arthur, however, the result of the earl's
mission to the duke, she returned to the palace,

C

and had induced her father to sign away his
kingdom, when his grandson Ferrand arrived
with the news of the rout of the Burgundian
army at Neufchatel, and Arthur learned from his
squire, Sigismund, that he had not seen Anne's
spectre but herself during his night-watch, and
that the priest he had met more than once was
her father, the Count Albert of Geierstein.   The
same evening Queen Margaret died in her chair
of state; and all the earl's prospects for England
being thwarted, he occupied himself in arranging a
treaty between her father and the King of France.

He was still in Provence when he was summoned
to rouse the duke from a fit of melancholy, caused
by the Switzers having again defeated him.   After
raising fresh troops, Charles decided to wrest Nancy
from the young Duke of Lorraine, and during the
siege Arthur received another challenge from
Rudolph.   The rivals met, and, having killed
the Bernese, the young Englishman obtained
Count Albert's consent to his marriage with
Anne, with strict injunctions to warn the duke
that the Secret Tribunal had decreed his death.
By the treachery of the Italians the Swiss were
enabled the same night to gain another victory,
Charles was slain, and their independence was
established.   Being still an exile, the earl accepted
the patriot Biederman's invitation to reside with
his countess at Geierstein, until the battle of Bos-
worth placed Henry VII. on the throne, when
Arthur and his wife attracted as much admiration
at the English Court as they had gained among
their Swiss neighbours.

THE MONASTERY

Principal Characters

WIDOW ELSPETH BRYDONE GLENDINNING, *of Glendearg.*

HALBERT, } *her sons.*
EDWARD, }

CAPTAIN STAWARTH BOLTON, *in command of English dragoons.*

BRITTSON, *his sergeant.*

WIDOW ALICE AVENEL, *of Eskdale.*

Her daughter, MARY.

JULIAN AVENEL, *her brother-in-law.*

MARTIN TACKET, *a shepherd.*

TIBB, *his wife.*

THE LORD ABBOT BONIFACE, *of St Mary's Monastery.*

FATHER PHILIP, *the sacristan.*

FATHER EUSTACE, *the sub-prior.*

CHRISTIE OF THE CLINTHILL, *a freebooter.*

HAPPER, *the miller.*

His daughter, MYSIE.

SIR PIERCIE SHAFTON, *an English courtier.*

REV. HENRY WARDEN, *a Protestant preacher.*

THE EARL OF MURRAY, *Regent of Scotland.*

LORD MORTON.

Spectre of the White Lady of Avenel, monks of St Mary's, vassals and neighbours, inhabitants of the village of Kennaquhair, English and Scottish soldiers.

Period, 1550. *Locality : Melrose on the Tweed and neighbourhood.*

IN the many conflicts between England and Scotland the property of the Church had hitherto always been respected ; but her temporal possessions, as well as her spiritual influence, were now in serious danger from the spread of the doctrines of the Reformation, and the occupants of the monasteries were dependent on the military services of their tenants and vassals for protection against the forays of Protestant barons and other heretical marauders. Dame Elspeth's hus-

band had fallen in the battle of Pinkie, and the
hospitality of her lonely tower had been sought
by the widow of the Baron of Avenel and her
daughter, whose mansion had been seized and
plundered by invaders, and subsequently taken
possession of by her brother-in-law. While con-
fessing the baroness on her death - bed, Father
Philip discovered that she possessed a Bible, and
as he was carrying it to the Lord Abbot, it was,
he declared, taken from him by a spectral White
Lady. Disbelieving the sacristan's tale, the sub-
prior visited the tower, where he met Christie of
the Clinthill, charged with an insolent message
from Julian Avenel, and learnt that the Bible
had been mysteriously returned to its owner.
Having exchanged it for a missal, he was unhorsed on his return by the apparition ; and, on
reaching the monastery, the book had disappeared
from his bosom, and he found the freebooter detained in custody on suspicion of having killed him.
The White Lady was next seen by Halbert, who
was conducted by her to a fairy grotto, where he
was allowed to snatch the Bible from a flaming altar.

During his absence from the tower the miller
and his daughter arrived on a visit, and soon afterwards Sir Piercie, as a refugee from the English
Court.   The next day the abbot came to dine with
them, and offered Halbert, who had quarrelled
with the knight for his attentions to Mary, the
office of ranger of the Church forests. He, however, refused it, and startled his rival with a token
he had obtained from the mysterious spectre. The
following morning they fought in a glen, and

Halbert fled to the Baron of Avenel, leaving Sir Piercie apparently mortally wounded. His companion thither was Henry Warden, who offended the laird, and assisted Halbert in his determination to escape from the castle, rather than serve under his host's standard. The knight, however, had miraculously recovered, and on making his way back to the tower, was accused by Edward of having murdered his missing brother, in spite of his assurance that the youth was alive and uninjured. With the sub-prior's approval he was treated as a prisoner; but during the night Mysie assisted him to escape, and accompanied him northwards, dressed as his page. Mary Avenel, meanwhile, in the midst of her grief at the supposed death of her lover, was visited by the White Lady, who comforted her by disclosing the place where he had hidden the Bible, which she had secretly read with her mother.

The rest of the family were astounded by the arrival of Christie, who confirmed Sir Piercie's assertion, and announced that he had brought Henry Warden to be dealt with as a heretic by the lord abbot. But the preacher and Father Eustace had been intimate friends at college, and the sub-prior was urging him to save his life by returning to the bosom of the Church, when Edward interrupted them to confess his jealousy of his brother, and his resolution to become a monk, in obedience to the White Lady who had appeared to him. Father Eustace then decided to leave his prisoner at the tower, under promise to surrender when summoned to the monastery;

and, having learnt from the freebooter that Julian
Avenel would fight for the Church, despatched him
in search of Sir Piercie and the miller's daughter.

That same night the lord abbot, alarmed by
intelligence that English and Scottish soldiers
were advancing with hostile intentions against the
monastery, resigned his office to the sub-prior.
Having taken the road to Edinburgh, Halbert
had joined a squadron commanded by the Earl
of Murray, who sent him forward to prevent an
engagement between the English, under Sir John
Forster, and the supporters of the Church, under
the Baron of Avenel. He arrived too late, but
the earl induced Sir John, who had won the battle,
to withdraw, and marched his troops to St Mary's.
Here the new abbot had assembled his brother-
hood in the village, in anticipation of the de-
struction of their home. The regent and his
followers formed up facing them, and the first
matter settled was the marriage of Halbert with
the heiress of Avenel. Father Eustace was then
summoned to produce Sir Piercie, who surrendered
voluntarily, and a flaw in his pedigree having
been proved, Mysie was declared a fitting wife
for him, and they were shipped off to Flanders.
The monks, at the intercession of Henry Warden,
were allowed to retain their monastery and lands
on condition of being laid under contribution;
while Edward, who had sought another interview
with the White Spirit, was told that the knot of
fate was tied, and impressed with the belief that
the marriage of his brother with Mary Avenel
might prove fatal to both of them.

THE ABBOT

Principal Characters

SIR HALBERT GLENDINNING, *of Avenel Castle, a Puritan.*
LADY GLENDINNING, *his wife.*
ROLAND GRÆME, *her page; afterwards* HEIR OF AVENEL.
MAGDALEN GRÆME, *his grandmother.*
REV. HENRY WARDEN, *a Puritan preacher.*
FATHER AMBROSE (*Edward Glendinning*), *Abbot of St Mary's.*
ADAM WOODCOCK, *Sir Halbert's falconer.*
LORD SEYTON, *an adherent of Mary Queen of Scots.*
His son, HENRY SEYTON.
His daughter, CATHERINE.

THE EARL OF MURRAY, *Regent of Scotland.*
LORD RUTHVEN, LORD LINDESAY, SIR ROBERT MELVILLE, *Lords of the Secret Council.*
SIR WILLIAM DOUGLAS, *of Lochleven Castle.*
THE LADY OF LOCHLEVEN, *his mother.*
LADY DOUGLAS, *his wife.*
GEORGE DOUGLAS, *their son.*
DRYFESDALE, *their steward.*
RANDAL, *their boatman.*
MARY QUEEN OF SCOTS.
LADY FLEMING, *her attendant.*
REV. ELIAS HENDERSON, *a Puritan chaplain.*

Lady Abbess, magistrates, halberdiers, citizens, boatmen, servants; contending Royalist and Presbyterian armies.

Period, 1567. *Locality : The Lowlands of Scotland.*

TEN years had passed away, during which Halbert had been knighted for his services to the regent, and Lady Avenel had adopted Roland, whom her dog had saved from drowning. The boy grew up petted by his mistress, but disliked by her chaplain and servants, and at length, having threatened to dirk the falconer, he was dismissed to seek his fortune. He had been secretly taught the Romish

39

faith by Father Ambrose, and led by his grandmother to believe that he was of gentle birth. She
now introduced him to Catherine Seyton, and then
accompanied him to the abbey, where the revels of
some masqueraders were interrupted by the arrival
of Sir Halbert on his way to Edinburgh, who
attached the youth to his train. On reaching the
capital he aided Lord Seyton in a street fray, and
was introduced to the Earl of Murray, who desired
him to be ready to travel at short notice. In
company with Adam Woodcock he adjourned to
an inn, and was entrusted by Henry Seyton (whom
he believed to be Catherine in male attire) with a
sword, which he was not to unsheath until commanded by his rightful sovereign. He then learnt
that he was to be attached to the household of
Queen Mary, and accompanied Lord Lindesay to
the castle of Lochleven, situated on an island,
where he found Catherine in attendance on her,
and was present when, in compliance with a note
contained in his sword-sheath, she signed her
abdication at the behest of the Secret Council.

After a lapse of several months, during which
Henderson attempted to convert him, Roland
learnt from Catherine that Father Ambrose had
been evicted from his monastery, and he pledged
himself, for her sake, to assist the imprisoned
queen in recovering her freedom. A plan of
escape arranged by George Douglas having failed
through the vigilance of the Lady of Lochleven,
Roland undertook to forge a false set of keys, and
the abbot arrived disguised as a man-at-arms sent
by Sir William to take part in guarding the castle.

As soon as the curfew had tolled, a preconcerted signal was made from the shore, and Roland contrived to substitute his forged keys for the real ones. At midnight the garden gate was unlocked, a boat was in waiting, Henry Seyton came forward, and the queen, with all her adherents, was safely afloat, when the alarm was given. Roland, however, had run back, ere they started, to turn the locks on their jailers, and, until they were out of reach of musketry, George Douglas protected Mary by placing himself before her. On landing, horses were in readiness, and before daybreak they reached Lord Seyton's castle in West Lothian, which was strongly garrisoned. The next morning, as the queen was endeavouring to make peace between Roland and Henry Seyton, who treated the page as a churl, his grandmother emerged from a recess and declared him to be the son of Julian Avenel, who was killed in the battle with Sir John Foster; Lord Seyton also recognised him, and insisted that his son should shake hands with him.

Supported by a considerable number of adherents in battle array, and accompanied by the abbot, the royal party moved onwards for Dumbarton, where help from France was expected. They were, however, intercepted by the regent's forces, and a desperate battle ensued. The queen stood near a yew tree, guarded by her devoted admirer George Douglas in close armour, while her page pushed forward to watch the conflict. It had lasted nearly an hour, when Sir Halbert attacked the flank of Mary's supporters, and they were completely routed, Henry Seyton was killed, and Douglas, who was mortally wounded, expired without withdrawing his eyes from her face. Hopeless of further aid, the queen adopted the fatal resolution of trusting to Elizabeth's mercy, and, having bid adieu to her followers, took ship for England. Roland soon afterwards succeeded in obtaining proofs of his claim as the heir of Avenel, and was married to Catherine on her return from two years residence with her unhappy mistress.

KENILWORTH

Principal Characters

GILES GOSLING, *host of the 'Black Bess,' at Cumnor.*

MICHAEL LAMBOURNE, *his nephew.*

MASTER TRESSILIAN, *a Cornish gentleman, Amy's lover.*

WAYLAND SMITH, *his servant.*

DUDLEY, EARL OF LEICESTER.

RICHARD VARNEY, *his squire.*

ANTHONY FOSTER, *steward of Cumnor Place.*

MASTER ERASMUS HOLIDAY, *a village pedagogue.*

DICKIE SLUDGE, *alias* FLIBBERTIGIBBET, *one of his pupils.*

DOCTOR DOBOOBIE, *alias* ALASCO, *an astrologer.*

SIR HUGH ROBSART, *of Lidcote Hall, Devonshire.*

His daughter, AMY.

JANET FOSTER, *her attendant at Cumnor.*

QUEEN ELIZABETH, *at Kenilworth.*

LORD HUNSDON,
LORD BURLEIGH,
SIR WALTER RALEIGH, } *In attendance on Her Majesty.*

Villagers and travellers at the inn, people on their way to the revels at Kenilworth, servants, etc.

Period, 1575. *Localities: Oxfordshire and Warwickshire.*

THE innkeeper had just welcomed his scape-grace nephew on his return from Flanders, and invited Tressilian and other guests to drink with them, when Lambourne made a wager he would obtain an introduction to a young lady under Foster's charge at the Hall, and the Cornish stranger begged permission to accompany him. On arriving there Tressilian found his lady-love, whom he would have carried back to her home, but she refused; and as he was leaving he encountered

43

Varney, whose life he might have taken had not
Lambourne intervened. Amy was soothed in her
seclusion by costly presents from the earl, and
during his next visit she pleaded that she might
inform her father of their secret marriage, but he
was afraid of Elizabeth's resentment. Warned by
his host against the squire, and having confided to
him how Amy had been entrapped, Tressilian left
Cumnor by night, and, after several adventures
by the way, reached the residence of Sir Hugh
Robsart, to assist him in laying his daughter's
case before the queen. Returning to London, his
servant, Wayland Smith, cured the Earl of Sussex
of a dangerous illness, on hearing of which from
Walter Raleigh, Elizabeth at once set out to visit
Leicester's rival, by whom the petition, in Amy's
behalf, was handed to her. Varney was accordingly summoned to the royal presence, when he
boldly declared that Amy was his wife, and
Leicester was restored to the queen's favour.

Tressilian's servant then gained access to the
countess as a pedlar, and, having hinted that
Elizabeth would shortly marry the earl, sold her
a cure for the heartache, warning Janet at the
same time against an attempt to poison her
mistress. Meanwhile Leicester was preparing to
entertain the queen at Kenilworth, where she had
commanded that Amy should be introduced to
her, and Varney was, accordingly, despatched with
a letter begging the countess to appear at the
revels as his bride. Having indignantly refused
to do so, and recovered from the effects of a
cordial which had been prepared for her by

Alasco, she escaped, with the help of her maid, from Cumnor, and started for Kenilworth, escorted by Wayland Smith. Travelling thither as brother and sister, they joined a party of mummers, and then, to avoid the crowd of people thronging the principal approaches, proceeded by circuitous by-paths to the castle. Having, with Dickie's help, passed into the courtyard, they were shown into a room, where Amy was waiting while her attendant carried a note to the earl, when she was startled by the entrance of her lover, whom she entreated not to interfere until after the expiration of twenty-four hours. On entering the park, Elizabeth was received by her favourite attended by a numerous cavalcade bearing waxen torches, and a variety of entertainments followed. During the evening she enquired for Varney's wife, and was told she was too ill to be present, when Tressilian offered to lose his head if within twenty-four hours he did not prove the statement to be false, notwithstanding which the ostensible bridegroom was knighted by the queen.

Receiving no reply to her note, which Wayland had lost, Amy found her way the next morning to a grotto in the gardens, where she was discovered by Elizabeth, who had just told her host that 'she must be the wife and mother of England alone.' Falling on her knees the countess besought protection against Varney, who she declared was not her husband, and added that the Earl of Leicester knew all. He was instantly summoned to the royal presence, and would have been committed to the Tower, had not Amy recalled her words, when she was consigned to Lord Hundson's care as bereft of her reason, Varney coming forward and pretending that she had just escaped from special treatment. Leicester insisted on an interview with her, when she implored him to confess their marriage to Elizabeth, and then, with a broken heart, she would not long darken his brighter prospects. Varney, however, succeeded in persuading him that Amy had acted in connivance with her lover, and in obtaining medical sanction for her custody as mentally disordered, asking only for the earl's signet-ring as his authority. The next day a duel between Tressilian and the earl was interrupted by Dickie, who produced the countess's note, and, convinced of her innocence, Leicester confessed that she was his wife. With the queen's permission he at once deputed his rival and Sir Walter Raleigh to proceed to Cumnor, whither he had already despatched Lambourne, to stay his squire's further proceedings.

Varney, however, had shot the messenger on receiving his instructions, and had caused Amy to be conducted by Foster to an apartment reached by a long flight of stairs and a narrow wooden bridge. The following evening the tread of a horse was heard in the courtyard, and a whistle like the earl's signal, upon which she rushed from the room, and the instant she stepped on the bridge, it parted in the middle, and—she was dead. Her murderer poisoned himself, and the skeleton of his accomplice was found, many years afterwards, in a cell where he secreted his

money. The news of the countess's fate put an
end to the revels at Kenilworth, Leicester retired
for a time from Court, and Sir Hugh Robsart,
who died very soon after his daughter, settled his
estate on Tressilian.

DEATH OF THE LAIRD'S JOCK

Principal Characters

JOHN ARMSTRONG, *the Laird of Mangertown.*
HIS SON.
HIS DAUGHTER.
FOSTER, *an English champion.*
Scottish and English Spectators.
Period, 1600. *Locality : Liddesdale in Roxburghshire.*

ARMSTRONG had been known during his father's
lifetime as the Laird's Jock, or son ; and being
possessed of great strength and courage, had distinguished himself in the use of a two-handed
sword, bequeathed to him by a Saxon outlaw,
in many of the single combats which took place
between the English and Scottish borderers during
the reign of Queen Elizabeth.

He had, however, grown old, and was bed-
ridden, when his only son accepted the challenge
of an English champion. But his heart swelled
with joy at the news, and having entrusted the
lad with his celebrated weapon, he insisted on
being wrapped in plaids and carried to the spot
selected for the encounter, attended by his
daughter. His followers gazed sadly on their
chieftain's withered features and shrunken form ;
but when the combatants met, and the English-

man brandished the sword over his fallen antagonist, the old laird, reanimated for an instant with
his former vigour, sprang from the rock on which
he was seated, and, having uttered a cry like that
of a dying lion rather than a human being, sank
into the arms of his clansmen broken-hearted, not
at the death of his boy, but at their wounded
honour, and the irreparable loss of his weapon.

THE FORTUNES OF NIGEL

Principal Characters

DAVID RAMSAY, *a watchmaker in Fleet Street.*
His daughter, MARGARET.
JENKIN VINCENT, \ *his ap-*
FRANCIS TUNSTALL, / *prentices.*
GEORGE HERIOT, *a goldsmith of Lombard Street.*
LORD GLENVARLOCH, *alias* NIGEL OLIFAUNT.
RICHIE MONOPLIES, *his servant.*
LAURENCE LINKLATER, *a yeoman of the royal kitchen.*
JOHN CHRISTIE, *a ship chandler.*
DAME NELLY, *his wife.*
BENJAMIN SUDDLECHOP, *a barber in Fleet Street.*
DAME URSULA, *his wife.*
KING JAMES I.
MAXWELL, *his gentleman usher.*
STEPHEN, DUKE of BUCKINGHAM.
LORD HUNTINGLEN.

LORD DALGARNO, *his son.*
REGINALD LOWESTOFFE, *a barrister.*
BEAUJEU, *host of a gambling tavern.*
SIR MUNGO MALLAGROWTHER, *a friend of Nigel's father.*
CHARLES, PRINCE OF WALES.
OLD TRAPBOIS, *a lodging-house keeper at Whitefriars.*
His daughter, MARTHA.
LADY HERMIONE ; *afterwards* LADY DALGARNO.
MONNA PAULA, *her servant.*
CAPTAIN COLEPEPPER, *a cutthroat adventurer.*
HILDEBROD, *a bailiff.*
THE GOVERNOR OF THE TOWER.
LADY MANSELL, *his wife.*
ANDREW SKURLIEWHITTER, *a scrivener.*

Courtiers and men of fashion, promenaders in the park, rangers and keepers, watermen, guards, servants, etc.

Period, 1604. *Localities: London, Greenwich and Enfield Chase.*

THE two apprentices had started off to join in a street fray, and Heriot was gossiping with Ramsay, when they brought in Monoplies with a broken head and very tattered garments. His wound having been dressed, he explained that he had

50

come to London with his master to obtain payment of a debt owing to him by the king, and had been set upon as a stranger. Next morning Nigel received a visit, at his lodging with the chandler and his wife, from the goldsmith, who had known his father, and, having warned him that his estate was in danger, lent him money to appear in proper attire in Court. Heriot proceeded to Whitehall, and, having presented the young lord's petition, James authorised him to advance part of the sum due, and promised to interest himself in his affairs. Dining with him the same day at the goldsmith's, in company with her father and Sir Mungo, Margaret lost her heart to Nigel, and employed Dame Ursula to ascertain all particulars respecting him. On being presented at Court by Lord Huntinglen he obtained an order for payment of his claim, and was introduced to the Duke of Buckingham, who announced himself as his enemy, and to Lord Dalgarno, by whom he was initiated in all the vices of the aristocracy of that period, although warned by Richie, and by an anonymous letter. Meeting the Prince of Wales in St James's Park, attended by several courtiers, Nigel learnt from their manner, as well as from Sir Mungo, that he had been ill spoken of to Charles, upon which he challenged Dalgarno in the precincts of the Court, and was compelled to take refuge in Whitefriars to avoid arrest.

Here he renewed his acquaintance with Lowestoffe, whom he had met at Beaujeu's, and was assigned to the care of old Trapbois and his

daughter. On hearing of Nigel's trouble Margaret
sought an interview with Lady Hermione, who
occupied a suite of apartments in Heriot's mansion, and, having revealed her secret, was supplied
with money to help him, being told at the same
time by her confidant of the ill usage she had
suffered from Lord Dalgarno. Vincent, who was
in love with his master's daughter, and had been
encouraged by Dame Ursula in extravagant habits,
was now engaged by her to act as his rival's guide
in effecting his escape from London. The same
night old Trapbois was murdered by two ruffians
who came to rob him ; and, just as he had rescued
the daughter, whom Hildebrod had advised him
to marry, Nigel was accosted by the apprentice,
dressed as a waterman, from whom he learnt that
a warrant had been issued for his apprehension,
and that a boat was in readiness for him to give
the king's officers the slip. Martha begged that
she might accompany him, and, having secured
her father's treasure, they were conducted by Vincent to the Temple Stairs. Having landed his
companion at Paul's Wharf, where she was taken
charge of by Monoplies, Nigel insisted on disem-
barking at Greenwich, instead of joining a Scotch
vessel which was waiting for him at Gravesend;
and having made his way to the park, he attended
the king while he killed a deer, when he was recognised and consigned to the Tower.

Presently Margaret, dressed as a boy, was shown
into the same room; then the chandler came to
claim his wife, whom he accused Nigel of having
carried off; and, after he had dined, his friend

Heriot arrived to reproach him with the position in which he had placed himself. He had also lost the king's warrant for his debt, and when his companion's disguise was detected, she saved him from further embarrassment by a full confession. One of her acts had been to present a petition to the king from Lady Hermione, on reading which he had commanded that Lord Dalgarno should instantly marry her ; and another to offer such explanations respecting Nigel as induced his Majesty to pardon him. One hour only, however, remained within which to redeem his estates, when Monoplies appeared with the money, and Lord Dalgarno, who hoped to have secured them, was deprived of his revenge. The next day he was shot in Enfield Chase, where Captain Colepepper had planned to waylay him, as he was waiting, in company w'th Dame Nelly, and a page in charge of the treasure, to fight a duel with Nigel. Vincent and Lowestoffe, however, arrived in time to put two of the robbers to flight, while Monoplies killed the captain, who was suspected of having murdered Trapbois, and Christie recovered his wife. Nigel and Margaret were soon afterwards married ; and as King James was honouring the feast with his presence, Richie presented Martha as his bride, who, at the same time, handed to the preserver of her life the deeds of the Glen-varloch estates, which she had freed from all liabilities, and the royal sign-manual which had been found among her father's papers.

A LEGEND OF MONTROSE

Principal Characters

THE YOUNG EARL OF MEN-
TEITH.
ANDERSON, *his servant; after-
wards* THE EARL OF MON-
TROSE.
SIR DUGALD DALGETTY, *of
Drumthwacket.*
ANGUS MACAULAY, *laird of
Kintail.*
His brother, ALLAN.
SIR MILES MUL-
GRAVE,
SIR CHRISTOPHER
HALL,
} *Guests of
Angus
MacAulay.*
THE CHILDREN OF THE MIST,
freebooters.

EVAN DHU, *a Highland chief-
tain.*
SIR DUNCAN CAMPBELL, *of
Ardenvohr, a Covenanter.*
ANNOT LYLE, *a harpist; after-
wards his daughter.*
MACCALLUM MORE, MARQUIS
OF ARGYLE.
RANALD MACEAGH, *a son of
the Mist.*
KENNETH, *his grandson.*
MACILDUY, *chieftain of the
Camerons.*

*Highland chieftains and clansmen, women and children;
Royalist army, Highland army.*

Period, 1645. *Localities:* ·*Various parts of Scotland.*

THE Civil War between Charles I. and his Parliament was raging in England; and, as the Earl of
Menteith was on his way to a political gathering
at Darnlinvarach Castle, he met Dalgetty, who
talked of his service as a soldier of fortune
abroad, and to whom he offered quarters for the
night, with the option of joining the Royalist
cause if he should feel so inclined. After supper
the earl related to the captain a story concerning
their guests, Angus and Allan MacAulay, whose
uncle having been murdered by a tribe of High-

landers called the Children of the Mist, the shock affected their mother's reason, and Allan inherited a gloomy and superstitious temperament, which Annot, who had been captured in one of their reprisals against the freebooters, and adopted by them, was in the habit of soothing with her harp. Dugald decided to take service on the king's side; and several chieftains and their followers having assembled at the castle, the Earl of Montrose, throwing off his disguise as a servant, accepted the command of the forces to be raised for the service of His Majesty in Scotland. As he was making his arrangements, Sir Duncan Campbell arrived to demand, in the Marquis of Argyle's name, an explanation of the meeting, and the captain was selected to return with him to Inverary to propose a truce.

After a halt at Sir Duncan's castle, Dalgetty was escorted to the stronghold of the Argyles, where he was received as the bearer of a traitorous message, and consigned to a dungeon. Here he found Ranald MacEagh, and had just learnt from him that Sir Duncan's daughter, whom he believed had been murdered, was alive, when they were interrupted by a stranger, who brought the captain some refreshment, and elicited from the Highlander that she was the little harpist. He then made dishonourable proposals to Dalgetty, but, recognising him as the marquis, the captain secured him, and escaped with Ranald, who undertook to guide him safely back to Montrose's headquarters. While crossing a dark ravine they heard the baying of a hound, and on reaching

the summit of the pass, where they were surrounded by the Children of the Mist, their pursuers overtook them. Their first assailant was
transfixed with an arrow, but the captain was
wounded, and carried away insensible by the
Highland women. In two battles which ensued,
the Covenanters were defeated by the Royalists,
and Montrose was hesitating as to his further
plans, when Dalgetty reappeared in his camp with
Ranald. The earl decided to avail himself of the
mountaineer's knowledge of Argyle's movements,
but, remembering the MacAulays' enmity against
his tribe, he was attached to the army under an
assumed name, and as a seer. Annot had followed
her protectors in the campaign, but now Allan became anxious for her safety, and possessed with a
foreboding that he was doomed to stab Menteith.

After considerable manœuvring on both sides,
Montrose was, at length, induced by MacIlduy to
make a sudden advance against Argyle, who
watched the battle from the deck of a galley.
The struggle was long and desperate, but the
Royalists gained the day, and, having been unhorsed by Ranald, Sir Duncan Campbell was
attacked by Allan MacAulay, who would have
killed him had not Dalgetty interposed. Montrose rode up in time to prevent a further scuffle,
and having knighted Sir Dugald, despatched him
and his antagonist in opposite directions. He
then cautioned the young Earl of Menteith
against his love for Annot, whom he could not
marry, and that he had a dangerous rival. She
was preparing dressings for the wounded, when

Allan suddenly entered the room, and, taxing her with reciprocating the earl's love, warned her that never was an injury offered him for which he exacted not tenfold vengeance. Sir Dugald now fetched her to examine Sir Duncan's wound, which she pronounced beyond her skill, when MacEagh begged that he might be allowed an interview with them, and revealed the secret that they were father and daughter. While Menteith was collecting the proofs of his statements, Ranald sent for his grandson, Kenneth, and despatched him with the news to MacAulay, enjoining the lad, with his dying breath, to pursue the wild life of his forefathers, to requite kindness, and avenge the injuries of his race.

Montrose still advised his kinsman to abandon the idea of making the old knight's heiress his wife, but Sir Duncan, having satisfied himself that her happiness depended on it, consented that they should be married, on the understanding that she returned to his castle until her husband could retire with honour from his military service. Everything was arranged accordingly, when Allan MacAulay presented himself in the ante-room of the chapel, and, having stabbed his rival in the breast, carried the reeking dirk to the Marquis of Argyle, and was never seen again. The earl recovered and was united to Annot, and Sir Dugald Dalgetty, having escaped the fate of his fellow-prisoners after the battle of Philiphaugh, consented, at the expiration of his engagement with the king, to take service with his enemies, and ultimately re-gained his paternal estate.

WOODSTOCK

Principal Characters

SIR HENRY LEE, of *Ditchley, keeper of Woodstock Park.*
His son, ALBERT, *a Royalist colonel.*
His daughter, ALICE.
DR ANTHONY ROCHECLIFFE, *late rector of Woodstock.*
REV. NEHEMIAH HOLDENOUGH, *a Presbyterian minister.*
COLONEL MARKHAM EVERARD, *a Roundhead, Sir Henry's nephew.*
JOCELINE JOLIFFE, *a Royalist forester, and Sir Henry's servant.*
PHŒBE MAYFLOWER, *his sweetheart.*

COLONEL DESBOROUGH,
GENERAL HARRISON,
JOSHUA BLETSON, } *Commissioners of the Council of State.*
JOSEPH TOMKINS, *their steward.*
CAPTAIN ROGER WILDRAKE, *of Squattlesea-mere.*
SPITFIRE, *his page.*
OLIVER CROMWELL.
CAPTAIN PEARSON, *his aide-de-camp.*
LOUIS KERNEGUY, *a page; afterwards* KING CHARLES II.
BEVIS, *a wolf-dog.*

Congregation in Woodstock Church, officers and soldiers of Cromwell's army, servants, etc.

Period, 1652. *Localities : Woodstock in Oxfordshire, and Windsor.*

AT a thanksgiving service in Woodstock church for the victory at Worcester, the Rev. Nehemiah Holdenough was compelled to cede the pulpit, which he had usurped from the late rector, to Tomkins, who, in military attire, declaimed against monarchy and prelacy, and announced the sequestration of the royal lodge and park by Cromwell and his followers. Proceeding thither, he

encountered Sir Henry, accompanied by Alice,
prepared to surrender his charge, and was conducted through the principal apartments by Joliffe,
who managed to send Phœbe and Bevis with some
provisions to his hut, in which the knight and
his daughter had arranged to sleep. On arriving
there they found Everard, who had come to offer
them his own and his father's protection; but Sir
Henry abused and spurned him as a rebel, and
at Alice's entreaty he bade them farewell, as he
feared, for ever. On his way to the lodge he met
his Royalist friend, Wildrake, whom he was sheltering in spite of his politics, and determined to send
him with an appeal to Cromwell to reinstate his
uncle at Woodstock. On reaching Windsor, the
captain, disguised as a Roundhead, obtained an
interview with the general, and a compliance with
Everard's request, on condition that he would aid
in securing the murdered king's son, in the event
of his seeking refuge with the Lees.

Armed with the warrant of ejectment, the colonel
and Wildrake, accompanied by the mayor and the
minister, visited the Commissioners during their
evening carouse, and took part in endeavouring
to ascertain the cause of some startling occur-
rences by which they had been disturbed. Everard
made his way alone to a dark gallery, in which he
fancied he heard his cousin's voice, and suddenly
felt a sword at his throat. Meeting Wildrake as
he regained the hall, they hurried off to the hut
where they found Dr Rochecliffe reading the
Church service to Sir Henry and his daughter;
and, after a reconciliation between uncle and

nephew, the cousins were allowed a private interview, during which Alice warned her lover against
betraying the king. Returning to the lodge they
were told of other unaccountable events; and
during the night Everard was ordered by an
apparition to change his quarters. The sentinels
also declared that they had heard strange sounds,
and the Commissioners decided to retire to the
village inn. Master Holdenough, too, confessed
that he had been terribly shocked by the reflec-
tion in a mirror of the figure of a college friend
whom he had seen drowned.

The following day the old knight was induced
to resume his post, and his son Albert arrived
with Louis Kerneguy, whom he introduced as his
Scotch page. Sir Henry having no suspicion who
his guest really was treated him without ceremony;
and while Dr Rochecliffe and the colonel were
planning for his escape to Holland, Charles amused
himself by endeavouring to gain Alice's love ; but,
in spite of a declaration of his rank, she made
him ashamed of his suit. A quarrel, however,
having arisen between him and Everard, she
evinced her loyalty by preventing a duel they
had arranged, at the risk of her reputation and
the loss of her cousin's affection. A similar
attempt by Tomkins to trifle with Phœbe was
punished by a death-blow from Joliffe. The next
evening Everard and his friend, and Holdenough,
were unexpectedly made prisoners by Cromwell,
who, having received intelligence of their knowledge of the king's sojourn at Woodstock, had
brought a large force to secure him. Wildrake,

however, managed to send warning to the lodge by Spitfire, and while Alice acted as Charles's guide to take horse, Albert, in his dress, concealed himself in Rosamond's tower. Cromwell and his soldiers arrived soon afterwards with Dr Rochecliffe and Joliffe, whom they had seized as they were burying Tomkins, and, having searched all the rooms and passages in vain, they proceeded to blow up the tower. Albert, however, leapt from it just before the explosion, and Cromwell was furious when he discovered the deception. In his rage he ordered the execution of the old knight and all his abettors, including his dog; but afterwards released them, with the exception of Albert, who was imprisoned, and subsequently fell in the battle of Dunkirk. Alice returned in safety, with the news that the king had effected his escape, and a letter from him to Sir Henry, approving of her marriage with Everard, whose political opinions had been considerably influenced by recent events.

Eight years later Wildrake arrived at Brussels with a message for Charles that his restoration had been voted by Parliament; and in his progress to London, escorted by a brilliant retinue, amidst shouts of welcome from his assembled subjects, he dismounted to salute a family group in which the central figure was the old knight of Ditchley, whose venerable features expressed his appreciation of the happiness of once more pressing his sovereign's hand, and whose death almost immediately followed the realisation of his anxious and long-cherished hopes.

PEVERIL OF THE PEAK

Principal Characters

SIR GEOFFREY PEVERIL, *of Martindale Castle, The Peak, Derbyshire.*
LADY MARGARET, *his wife.*
JULIAN, *their son.*
LANCE OUTRAM, *their gamekeeper.*
MAJOR BRIDGENORTH, *of Moultrassie Hall, a Puritan.*
His daughter, ALICE.
DEBORAH DEBBITCH, *her nurse.*
REV. NEHEMIAH SOLSGROVE, *a Presbyterian minister.*
CHARLOTTE, COUNTESS OF DERBY.
THE YOUNG EARL, *her son.*
EDWARD CHRISTIAN, *alias* RICHARD GANLESSE, *a Dempster of Man.*

FENELLA, *alias* ZARAH, *his daughter.*
CHARLES TOPHAM, *officer of the Black Rod.*
CHIFFINCH, *alias* WILL SMITH, *servant to Charles II.*
MISTRESS CHIFFINCH.
VILLIERS, DUKE OF BUCKINGHAM.
JERNINGHAM, *his secretary.*
KING CHARLES II.
MASTER MAULSTATUTE, *a Justice.*
SIR GEOFFREY HUDSON, *the Queen's Dwarf.*
COLONEL BLOOD, *an adventurer.*
THE DUKE OF ORMOND.

Servants, innkeepers, Roundheads, miners, watermen, constables, judge and jury, witnesses, conspirators and musicians.

Period, 1678. *Localities ; Derbyshire, Isle of Man and London.*

SIR GEOFFREY and Bridgenorth had been boys together ; and although they adopted different views in religion and politics, the major's influence had saved the Royalist's life after the battle of Bolton-le-Moor, and Lady Peveril had brought up his motherless girl with her own son. After the Restoration, the Countess of Derby, who, through treachery, had suffered a long imprisonment by the Roundheads, sought protection at Martindale Castle, where Bridgenorth would have arrested her for having caused his brother-in-law, William Christian, to be shot as a traitor, had not the knight interfered by tearing up the warrant, and escorting her through Cheshire on her return to the Isle of Man. Alice was of course withdrawn from his wife's care, and it was supposed the major had emigrated to New England. Several years afterwards Julian became the companion of the young earl, and, with Deborah's connivance, renewed his intimacy with his foster sister, who was under the care of her widowed aunt, Dame Christian. At one of the secret interviews between them, they were surprised by the entrance of her father, who related some of his religious experiences, and vaguely hinted that his consent to their marriage was not impossible. The next night, having undertaken to proceed to London, to clear the countess and her son from the suspicion of being concerned in Oates's pretended Popish plot, Julian was conducted to a sloop by Fenella, his patron's deaf and dumb dwarf, and, as she was being taken ashore against her will while he was asleep, he dreamt that he heard Alice's voice calling for his help.

At Liverpool he met Topham with a warrant against Sir Geoffrey, and on his way to the Peak to warn him, he travelled with Edward Christian, passing as Ganlesse, a priest, who led him to an inn, where they supped with Chiffinch. On reaching Martindale Castle, he found his father and mother in the custody of Roundheads, and he was

taken by Bridgenorth as a prisoner to Moultrassie
Hall, where Alice received them, and he recognised Ganlesse among a number of Puritan visitors.
During the night the Hall was attacked by the
dependents and miners of the Peveril estate, and,
having regained his liberty, Julian started, with
Lance as his servant, in search of his parents,
who he ascertained were on their way to London
in charge of Topham. At an inn where they
halted, Julian overheard Chiffinch revealing to a
courtier a plot against Alice, and that he had
been robbed of the papers entrusted to him by
the countess, which, however, he managed to
recover the next morning.

Meanwhile, Christian, under whose care Bridgenorth had placed his daughter, communicated to
the Duke of Buckingham a design he had formed
of introducing her to Charles II., and, at an interview with her father, endeavoured to persuade him
to abandon the idea of marrying her to young
Peveril.   Having reached London, Julian met
Fenella, who led him into St James's Park, where
she attracted the notice of the king by dancing,
and he sent them both to await his return at
Chiffinch's apartments. Alice was already under
the care of Mistress Chiffinch, and escaped from
an interview with the duke to find herself in the
presence of Charles and her lover, with whom,
after he had placed the countess's papers in the
king's hands, she was allowed to depart. Julian,
however, lost her in a street fray, and having
been committed to Newgate for wounding his
assailant, he was placed in the same cell with

the queen's dwarf, and conversed with an invisible speaker. After startling Christian with the news that his niece had disappeared, the duke bribed Colonel Blood to intercept his movements, so that he might not discover where she was, and was then himself astonished at finding Fenella instead of Alice, who had been captured by his servants in his house, and at her equally unexpected defiance of and escape from him.

A few days afterwards, Sir Geoffrey Peveril, his son and the dwarf were tried for aiding and abetting Oates's Plot, and were all acquitted. In order, however, to avoid the mob, they took refuge in a room, where they encountered Bridgenorth, who convinced Julian that they were in his power, and allowed Christian to propose to the Duke of Buckingham that several hundred Fifth-Monarchy men, led by Colonel Blood, should seize the king, and proclaim his Grace Lord-Lieutenant of the kingdom. The same afternoon Charles had just granted an audience to the Countess of Derby, when the dwarf emerged from a violoncello case and revealed the conspiracy which Fenella had enabled him to overhear. It then transpired that Bridgenorth had released the Peverils, and that Christian had trained his daughter, whose real name was Zarah, to feign being deaf and dumb, in order that she might act as his spy; but that her secret love for Julian had frustrated the execution of his vengeance against the countess. He was allowed to leave the country, and the major, who, on recovering Alice by Fenella's aid, had placed her under Lady Peveril's care, having

E

offered to restore some of Sir Geoffrey's domains which had passed into his hands as her dowry, the king's recommendation secured the old knight's consent to the marriage which within a few weeks united the Martindale - Moultrassie families and estates.

OLD MORTALITY

Principal Characters

MR MORTON, *the Squire of Milnwood, a Presbyterian.*
HENRY MORTON, *his nephew.*
DAME ALISON WILSON, *his housekeeper.*
LADY MARGARET BELLENDEN, *of Tullietudlem.*
Her grand-daughter, EDITH.
MAJOR BELLENDEN, *her brother-in-law, a Cavalier.*
GUYDILL, *her butler.*
JENNY DENNISON, *Edith's maid.*
LORD EVANDALE.
LADY EMILY HAMILTON, *his sister.*
FRANCIS STEWART, *alias* BOTHWELL, *sergeant of Claverhouse's Life Guards.*
TAM HALLIDAY, *his comrade.*
JOHN BALFOUR OF BURLEY, *a Covenanter.*
CORNET GRAHAM, *a kinsman of Claverhouse.*

MAUSE HEADRIGG, *an old fanatic.*
CUDDIE, *her son, a ploughman.*
COLONEL GRAHAM OF CLAVERHOUSE, *afterwards* VISCOUNT OF DUNDEE.
GABRIEL KETTLEDRUMLE, POUNDTEXT, MACBRIAR, } *Covenant preachers.*
THE DUKE OF MONMOUTH, *commander of the English army.*
GENERAL DALZELL, *his aide-de-camp.*
MUCKLEWRAITH, *a fanatic.*
DUKE OF LAUDERDALE, *President of Council at Edinburgh.*
BASIL OLIFANT, *a renegade Covenanter.*
BESSIE MACCLURE, *a blind widow.*
WITTENBOLD, *commander of Dutch Dragoons.*

Army of rebel Whigs, English and Scotch soldiers, procession through the streets of Edinburgh, servants, etc.

Period, 1679. *Localities: Scotland and Holland.*

'OLD MORTALITY' was a native of Dumfries, who devoted himself, for many years, to restoring the gravestones of the Covenanters who had suffered during the religious persecutions in the seventeenth century, and he furnished the author with many of the incidents upon which this tale is founded.

Henry Morton had beaten Lord Evandale in
shooting at the figure of a bird called a popinjay,
in the presence of all the aristocracy of Lanarkshire, and was entertaining his companions at the
village inn, where Bothwell and Halliday insisted
on Balfour toasting the archbishop. Having done
so with a qualification, he overpowered the sergeant in a wrestle, and rode away with Morton,
whose father's life he had saved. Shortly afterwards the cornet arrived with the news that the
primate had been murdered, and in search of the
Covenanter, who, however, was warned by Bessie
MacClure to defer proceeding on his journey, and
passed the night in a loft at Milnwood, where,
at Edith's request, Cuddie and his mother were
afforded shelter from the bigotry of her grandmother. Next day the red-coats came to arrest
Henry for sheltering Balfour, and carried him to
Lady Bellenden's castle, to be dealt with by
Claverhouse, who ordered him to be shot; but
Edith entreated Lord Evandale's intercession, and
her lover's life was spared. Information had been
received of a large gathering of armed Whigs in
the neighbourhood, and, during a fierce encounter
between them and the Royalist troops, Balfour shot
the cornet, and transfixed Bothwell with his sword,
upon which Claverhouse charged the rebels and
unhorsed the Covenanter. The king's forces, however, were compelled to retire, and Lord Evandale's
life was saved by Morton, who took service under
Balfour.

A detachment of the insurgents now invested
the castle of Tullietudlem, while Henry marched

with the main body against Glasgow, which the
Royalists evacuated in order to reach Edinburgh,
where the Duke of Monmouth was commander-in-
chief. He managed, however, to get back to
Milnwood, and, having rescued Lord Evandale
from hanging, employed him to suppress a mutiny
among the troopers in the castle, and to induce
Major Bellenden to surrender it, on the promise
of a safe-conduct in charge of a petition to the
Government. While Balfour was making free
with Lady Bellenden's property, Morton obtained
a fruitless audience at the duke's camp, and returned to prepare the rebel army for battle, instead
of listening to their Cameronian preachers. In the
fight which ensued, the king's forces prevailed,
Balfour was disabled, and all Henry's efforts to
rally the Covenanters having failed, he and his
servant Cuddie escaped with their lives, and
reached a solitary farmhouse. Here a party of
fanatical western Whigs had assembled, and Morton,
having been denounced by Macbriar and Mucklewraith as a prelatist, was sentenced to die at midnight. Ere that hour arrived, however, Claverhouse
and a party of soldiers forced an entrance, and he
became their prisoner. From a window at Edinburgh he witnessed the triumphant entry of the
royal troops with their prisoners, preceded by the
civil authorities, and followed by an excited mob.
He was then summoned to the council chamber,
and, on pledging himself to remain abroad during
the king's pleasure, he was pardoned, Claverhouse
accompanying him to Leith, where he embarked
for Holland.

Nine years afterwards, on revisiting the old neighbourhood, he learnt that Olifant, a discarded suitor for the heiress, was in possession of the Bellenden estate, and that Edith was betrothed to his rival. He was urging her to consent to their marriage before he joined the Scottish rising against William III., when she declared that she had seen her lost lover, and was taken dangerously ill. Balfour was hiding in a cavern near the widow MacClure's cottage, and, at an interview with him, Morton saved himself with difficulty from his religious frenzy. As he returned he overheard a plot to surprise Lord Evandale ; and, while he was on his way to Glasgow to obtain military aid, a party of horsemen, headed by Olifant, approached the mansion where his lordship was taking leave of Edith, in despair of gaining her affection. Followed by his servants he rode to meet them, and fell from his horse mortally wounded. The renegade was killed at the same time, and as Balfour was attacking Halliday, a troop of Dutch dragoons came to the rescue. All the assailants surrendered except the Covenanter, who was pursued, and, after a desperate struggle, was drowned with one of the soldiers in his grasp. Lord Evandale, as he was dying, joined Edith's and Morton's hands, and Lady Margaret recovered her castle and lands.

THE BRIDE OF LAMMERMOOR

Principal Characters

EDGAR, *heir of the late Master of Ravenswood.*
CALEB BALDERSTON, *his steward at Wolf's Crag Tower.*
MYSIE, *Caleb's wife.*
SIR WILLIAM ASHTON, *the Scottish Lord Keeper.*
LADY ASHTON, *his wife.*
SHOLTO DOUGLAS ASHTON,
HENRY ASHTON, } *their sons.*
Their daughter, LUCY.

AILSIE GOURLAY, *her nurse.*
CAPTAIN CRAIGENFELT, *a Jacobite adventurer.*
FRANK HAYSTON, *laird of Bucklaw.*
LADY GERNINGTON, *his aunt.*
LADY BLEKENSOP, *his kinswoman.*
ALICE, *a blind servant of the Ravenswood family.*
REV. MR BIDE-THE-BENT, *a Presbyterian minister.*

Funeral procession, foresters, servants, grave-diggers, villagers, surgeon and physicians.

Period, 1695. *Locality: East Lothian.*

THE ancient seat of the Ravenswood family had been purchased by Sir William Ashton, and the late lord, who was under attaint as a Jacobite, had inspired his son with a hatred towards him, which was enhanced by the lord keeper granting a warrant to prevent the use of the Episcopalian service at his father's funeral. The next day, as Sir William and his daughter were returning from a visit to old Alice, they were pursued by a bull, which was shot by Edgar, who carried Lucy to a fountain, but declined her father's thanks. He had

arranged to seek his fortune abroad with Bucklaw
and the captain, but, on meeting them at an inn,
he announced that he had changed his mind, and
invited the young laird to Wolf's Crag. Here
Caleb and Mysie made amusing efforts to maintain
their master's hospitality with a very slender stock
of provisions; and were still more disconcerted
when he returned home from a stag hunt with the
lord keeper and his daughter, to whom he had
offered shelter from a storm. The old steward,
however, managed by a ruse to shut the gates
against the huntsmen, who were entertained by
Bucklaw and Craigenfelt; and having abstracted
some wild fowl from a neighbour's spit, and pro-
cured other supplies, he was able to set a credit-
able meal before the guests, who passed the night
in the tower.

Sir William had been troubled with serious fears
of Edgar's inherited resentment, but they were
dissipated by his evident admiration of Lucy, and
his acceptance, in spite of Caleb's remonstrances,
of an invitation to spend a few days at Ravenswood. During this visit he was taken by Lucy
and her brother Henry to see old Alice, who
warned him that he came either in fatal anger or
in fatal love; but instead of saying farewell for
ever, as he had resolved, her tears prevailed, and
their troth was plighted to each other. Lady
Ashton, however, had arranged a match for her
daughter with Bucklaw, who had just inherited
his aunt's fortune, and, on returning home, wrote a
note to Edgar which left him no alternative but
to quit the house at once. On his way through

the park he encountered an apparition of old
Alice, and, on reaching her cottage, he found that
she had died a short time previously, expressing
an eager desire to speak to him.   Having received
an evasive reply from Sir William, and an insolent
one from her ladyship, to the letters he addressed
to them, and a few lines assuring him of her con-
stancy from Lucy, Ravenswood departed on a
mission abroad which his kinsman, the Marquis of
A., had confided to him.

During his absence Lady Ashton extorted a
promise from her daughter that she would marry
Bucklaw, on condition that Edgar released her, or
failed to answer the letter she had sent him, by
St Jude's day.   In the meantime she learnt that
the marquis was exerting his power to reverse
the judgments by which her father had become
possessed of the Ravenswood property, and was
told that Edgar, whose reply her mother had intercepted, was engaged to another lady.   Her
nurse had also filled her mind with melancholy
forebodings, and on Bucklaw presenting himself
again, at the expiration of the interval she had
agreed to, Lucy had just signed the marriage con-
tract, when the tramp of a horse was heard at the
gate, and she exclaimed, ' He is come ! '   Edgar
forced his way into the room, and having been
assured by the minister that she had executed the
deed without fraud or compulsion, he placed before
her their written engagement, with the portion he
had retained of the coin they had broken, and, at
his request, she returned him the tokens in her
possession.   Her mother determined that the

wedding with Bucklaw should take place on the appointed day, and Henry was censured for having lost the dagger he should have worn on the the occasion.   In the midst of the ball which followed their marriage, a piercing cry was heard, the bridegroom had been stabbed, and the bride was crouching in the chimney corner bereft of her reason.   She died the following evening ; and, on recovering from his wound, her husband declared he had neither story to tell nor injury to avenge. Ravenswood attended the funeral in disguise ; and, having accepted a challenge from Colonel Ashton, was riding to meet him, when he disappeared in the sand knolls he was crossing, the only vestige of his fate being the sable feather he had worn in his hat.

THE PIRATE

Principal Characters

MR BASIL MERTOUN, *alias* VAUGHAN, *of Jarlshof Castle, Sumburgh Head.*
His son, MORDAUNT.
SWERTHA, *their housekeeper.*
SWEYN ERICKSON, *a fisherman.*
MAGNUS TROIL, *a Zetland udaller, or landholder.*
MINNA, } *his daughters.*
BRENDA, }
EUPHANE FEA, *his housekeeper.*
ERIC SCAMBESTER, *his servant.*
ULLA TROIL, *alias* NORNA, *of the Fitful Head, his kinswoman.*
NICHOLAS STRUMPFER, *alias* PACOLET, *her servant.*

NEIL RONALDSON, *Ranzelman of Jarlshof.*
MR TRIPTOLEMUS YELLOWLEY, *of Harfra-Stourburgh, a Scotch factor.*
His sister, BARBARA.
TRONDA DRONSDAUGHTER, *their servant.*
BRYCE SNAILSFOOT, *a pedlar.*
CLAUD HALCRO, *an old bard.*
CLEMENT CLEVELAND, *alias* VAUGHAN, *a pirate captain.*
JOHN BUNCE, *alias* FREDERICK ALTAMONT, *his lieutenant.*
CAPTAIN WEATHERPORT, *of H.M.S. 'Halcyon.'*

Inhabitants of Shetland, guests at Burgh-Westra, masquers, provost and citizens of Kirkwall and Stromness, pirate officers and seamen.

Period, 1700. *Localities: Shetland and Orkney Islands.*

MR MERTOUN and his son had arrived as strangers, and resided for several years in the old mansion of the Earls of Orkney, the father leading a very secluded life, while Mordaunt became a general favourite with the inhabitants, and especially with the udaller and his daughters. On his way home from a visit to them, he and the pedlar sought shelter from a storm at the Yellowleys' farmhouse,

75

where they were amused with their penurious ways,
and encountered Norna, who was supposed to be
in league with the fairies, and to possess supernatural powers. The next day a ship was wrecked
on the rocky coast, and, at the risk of his life,
Mordaunt rescued Cleveland as he was cast on the
beach clinging to a plank, while Norna prevented
his sea-chest from being pillaged. The captain
promised his preserver a trip in a consort ship
which he expected would arrive shortly, and went
to seek the udaller's help in recovering some of
his other property that had been washed ashore.
After the lapse of several weeks, however, during
which the Troils had discontinued their friendly
communications with him, Mordaunt heard that
the stranger was still their guest, and that they
were arranging an entertainment for St John's Eve,
to which he had not been bidden.

As he was brooding over this slight, Norna
touched his shoulder, and, assuring him of her
goodwill, advised him to join the party uninvited.
Warned by his father against falling in love, and
with some misgivings as to his reception, he called
at Harfra on his way, and accompanied the factor
and his sister to the feast. Minna and Brenda
replied to their discarded companion's greeting
with cold civility, and he felt convinced that Cleveland had supplanted him in their esteem. The
bard endeavoured to cheer him with his poetry and
reminiscences of Dryden; and, in the course of
the evening, Brenda, disguised as a masquer, told
him they had heard that he had spoken unkindly
of them, but that she did not believe he had done

so. She also expressed her fear that the stranger
had won Minna's love, and begged Mordaunt to
discover all he could respecting him. During an
attempt to capture a whale the following day,
Cleveland saved Mordaunt from drowning, and,
being thus released from his obligation to him,
intimated that henceforth they were rivals. The
same evening the pedlar brought tidings that a
strange ship had arrived at Kirkwall, and Cleveland talked of a trip thither to ascertain whether it
was the consort he had been so long expecting.

After the sisters had retired to bed, Norna
appeared in their room, and narrated a startling
tale of her early life, which led Minna to confess her attachment to the captain, and to elicit
Brenda's partiality for Mordaunt. At a secret
interview the next morning, Cleveland admitted
to Minna that he was a pirate, upon which she
declared that she could only still love him as a
penitent, and not as the hero she had hitherto
imagined him to be. He announced, in the presence of her father and sister, his intention of starting at once for Kirkwall ; but at night he serenaded
her, and then, after hearing a struggle and a groan,
she saw the shadow of a figure disappearing with
another on his shoulders. Overcome with grief
and suspense, she was seized with a fit of melancholy, for the cure of which the udaller consulted
Norna in her secluded dwelling ; and, after a
mystic ceremony, she predicted that the cause
would cease when ' crimson foot met crimson hand'
in the Martyr's Aisle in Orkney land, whither she
commanded her kinsman to proceed with his

daughters. Mordaunt had been stabbed by the pirate, but had been carried away by Norna to Hoy, where she told him she was his mother, and, after curing his wound, conveyed him to Kirkwall. Here Cleveland had joined his companions, and, having been chosen captain of the consort ship, he obtained leave from the provost for her to take in stores at Stromness and quit the islands, on condition that he remained as a hostage for the crew's behaviour.

On their way they captured the brig containing the Troils, but Minna and Brenda were sent safely ashore by Bunce, and escorted by old Halcro to visit a relative. The lovers met in the cathedral of St Magnus, whence, with Norna's aid, Cleveland escaped to his ship, and the sisters were transferred to the residence of the bard's cousin, where their father joined them, and found Mordaunt in charge of a party of dependents for their protection. When all was ready for sailing, the captain resolved to see Minna once more, and having sent a note begging her to meet him at the Standing Stones at daybreak, he made his way thither. Brenda persuaded Mordaunt to allow her sister to keep the appointment, and as the lovers were taking their last farewell, they and Brenda were seized by Bunce and his crew from the boat, and would have been carried off, had not Mordaunt hastened to the rescue, and made prisoners of the pirate and his lieutenant. Norna had warned Cleveland against delaying his departure, and his last hopes were quenched when, from the window of the room in which he and Bunce were confined, they witnessed the arrival of the *Halcyon*, whose captain she had communicated with, and the capture, after a desperate resistance, of their ship.

The elder Mertoun now sought Norna's aid to save their son, who, he declared, was not Mordaunt, as she imagined, but Cleveland, whom he had trained as a pirate under his own real name of Vaughan, her former lover ; and having lost trace of him till now, had come to Jarlshof, with his child by a Spanish wife, to atone for the misdeeds of his youth. On inquiry it appeared that Cleveland and Bunce had earned their pardon by acts of mercy in their piratical career, and were allowed to enter the king's service. Minna was further consoled by a penitent letter from her lover; Brenda became Mordaunt's wife ; and the aberration of mind, occasioned by remorse at having caused her father's death, having passed away, Norna abandoned her supernatural pretensions and peculiar habits, and resumed her family name.

MY AUNT MARGARET'S MIRROR

Principal Characters

SIR PHILIP FORESTER.
His wife, LADY JEMIMA.
His wife's sister, LADY BOTH-
WELL.

MAJOR FALCONER, *their brother.*
BAPTISTA DAMIOTTI, *a Paduan
doctor.*

Servants, a physician.
Period, 1702. *Localities: Edinburgh and Flanders.*

SIR PHILIP, who had married for money and
quarrelled with his brother-in-law, determined to
join the Duke of Marlborough's army in Flanders
as a volunteer. Receiving no tidings of him for
many months, Lady Jemima resolved to consult a
doctor from Padua, who had the reputation of
being able to show his visitors their absent friends,
and what they were doing. Accordingly she and
her sister, disguised as soldiers' wives, went to him
secretly, when he at once told them their real
names and the information they desired. Having
enjoined absolute silence, and changed his dress to
that of an eastern necromancer, he led them into
a room hung with black and lighted with torches,
containing a large mirror behind an altar, on which
were two swords, an open book, and a human
skull. Gradually the mirror ceased to reflect these
objects, and they saw the interior of a foreign

church, in which Sir Philip was about to be
married to a beautiful girl, when a group of
officers entered, one of whom advanced towards
the bridal party, and swords were drawn on both
sides. The scene ·then vanished, and the mirror
again reflected the contents of the room. Restora-
tives were now offered to the ladies, and they were
conducted to their carriage, the professor handing
Lady Bothwell a composing draught for her sister.

A few days afterwards news arrived from
Holland that Sir Philip's nuptials with the
daughter of a rich burgo-master were actually
about to be celebrated, when Major Falconer,
who happened to be in the town, and had come
with some brother officers to witness the ceremony
as an amusement, recognised and denounced the
would-be bigamist, accepted a challenge from him,
and was killed. Lady Jemima never recovered
from the shock, the Italian disappeared to escape
arrest as a Jacobite, and Sir Philip having, in his
old age, sought in vain a reconciliation with Lady
Bothwell, eluded pursuit as a murderer and died
abroad.

F

THE BLACK DWARF

Principal Characters

HOBBIE ELLIOT, *of the Heugh-foot farm.*
HIS GRANDMOTHER.
OLD ANNAPPLE, *his foster mother.*
LILIAS,
JEAN,   } *his sisters.*
ANNOT,
GRACE ARMSTRONG, *his cousin and sweetheart.*
PATRICK EARNSCLIFF, *a young squire.*
ELSHIE, *the Dwarf of Mucklestane Moor; afterwards* SIR EDWARD MAULEY.

MR RICHARD VERE, *the laird of Ellislaw.*
His daughter, ISABEL.
SIR FREDERICK LANGLEY, *her suitor.*
LUCY ILDERTON, *her friend.*
WILLIE GRÆME, *of Westerburnflat, a freebooter.*
MR HUBERT RATCLIFFE, *a friend of Sir William Mauley.*
RALPH MARESCHAL, *Mr Vere's cousin.*
DR HOBBLER, *a priest.*

Elliot's brothers and neighbours, Westerburnflat's mother and comrades, Jacobite friends and servants of Mr Vere.

Period, 1706. *Locality : the Lowlands of Scotland.*

As Elliot was returning over a wild moor from a day's sport, thinking of the legends he had heard of its supernatural occupants after nightfall, he was overtaken by Earnscliff, whose father had been killed in a quarrel with the laird of Ellislaw, when the moon suddenly revealed the figure of a human dwarf, who, on being spoken to, refused their offers of assistance, and bid them begone. Having invited Earnscliff to sup with his women folks, and pass the night at his farm, Hobbie

accompanied him next morning to confront the
strange being by daylight; and having assisted
him in collecting stones for constructing a hut,
they supplied him with food and other necessaries.
In a short time he had completed his dwelling,
and became known to the neighbours, for whose
ailments he prescribed, as Elshender the Recluse.
Being visited by Isabel and two of her friends, he
told their fortunes, and he gave her a rose, with
strict injunctions to bring it to him in her hour of
adversity. As they rode homewards, their conversation implied that she loved young Earnscliff,
but that Mr Vere intended her to marry Sir
Frederick. Another of his visitors was Westburnflat, on his way to avenge an affront he had
received from Elliot, whose dog the next day
killed one of the dwarf's goats, for which he
warned him that retribution was at hand.

Shortly afterwards the freebooter brought word
that he and his companions had fired Hobbie's
farm, and carried off his sweetheart and cattle;
on hearing which Elshie despatched him with an
order for some money, and insisted that Grace
should be given up uninjured. Having dispersed
his neighbours in search of her, Elliot went to consult Elshie, who handed him a bag of gold, which
he declined, and intimated that he must seek her
whom he had lost in the *west*. Earnscliff and his
party had tracked the cattle as far as the English
border, but on finding a large Jacobite force assembling there they returned, and it was decided
to attack Westburnflat's stronghold. On approaching it, a female hand, which her lover swore was

Grace's, waved a signal to them from a turret, and
as they were preparing a bonfire to force the
door, Græme agreed to release his prisoner, who
proved to be Isabel.   On reaching home, however,
Elliot found his cousin had been brought back, and
at dawn he started off to accept the money which
the dwarf had offered him to repair his homestead.
Isabel had been seized by ruffians while walking
with her father, who appeared overcome with grief,
and under the impression that Earnscliff was the
offender ; whereas Mr Ratcliffe, who managed his
affairs, suggested that Sir Frederick had stronger
motives for placing her under restraint.   Mr Vere's
suspicion seemed justified by their meeting his
daughter returning under her lover's care ; but she
confirmed his version of the circumstances under
which he had intervened, to the evident discom-
fiture of his rival and her father.

At a large gathering, the same day, of the Pretender's adherents in the hall of Ellieslaw Castle,
Mareschal produced a letter which dissipated all
their hopes, and Sir Frederick insisted that his
marriage with Isabel should take place before
midnight.   She had consented, on her father's
representation that his life would be forfeited if
she refused, when Mr Ratcliffe persuaded her to
make use of the token which Elshie had given her,
and escorted her to his dwelling.   He promised
that at the foot of the altar he would redeem her ;
and, just as the ceremony was commencing in the
chapel, a voice, which seemed to proceed from her
mother's tomb, uttered the word 'Forbear.'   The
dwarf s real name and rank were then revealed, as

well as the circumstances under which he had
acquired the power of thus interfering on Isabel's
behalf; while Hobbie and his friends supported
Mr Ratcliffe in dispersing the would-be rebels.
Sir Edward at the same time disappeared from
the neighbourhood, and Mr Vere retired, with an
ample allowance, to the Continent, all the Ellieslaw
property, as well as the baronet's, being settled on
Earnscliff and his bride. Sir Frederick Langley
was, a few years afterwards, executed at Preston,
and Westburnflat earned a commission in Marlborough's army by his services in providing cattle
for the commissariat.

ROB ROY

Principal Characters

MR WILLIAM OSBALDISTONE, *of the firm of Osbaldistone & Tresham.*
FRANK OSBALDISTONE, *his son.*
MR OWEN, *principal clerk to the firm.*
ANDREW FAIRSERVICE, *Frank's servant.*
SIR FREDERICK VERNON, *a Jacobite.*
His daughter, DIANA.
SIR HILDEBRAND OSBALDISTONE, *his maternal uncle.*
RASHLEIGH OSBALDISTONE, *his son.*
MARTHA, *Diana's maid.*
SQUIRE INGLEWOOD, *a Northumbrian justice of the peace.*
MR JOSEPH JOBSON, *his clerk.*

MACVITTIE & MACFIN, *traders in Glasgow.*
DOUGAL, *a turnkey in the Tolbooth.*
BAILIE NICOL JARVIE, *a weaver.*
MATTIE, *his servant.*
JEAN MACALPINE, *hostess f inn at Aberfoil.*
MAJOR GALBRAITH, *of the Lennox militia.*
MACSTUART, *one of his troopers.*
CAPTAIN THORNTON, *of the Royals.*
ROB ROY MACGREGOR CAMPBELL, *a Scottish outlaw.*
His wife, HELEN.
ROBERT, } *their sons.*
HAMISH, }

Highlanders and soldiers, servants, etc.

Period, 1715. *Localities: Northumberland, Glasgow and neighbourhood.*

FRANK OSBALDISTONE had declined a partnership in his father's business; and as he was journeying nothwards, on a visit to his uncle Sir Hildebrand, he travelled with a very nervous man, and dined at an inn with Mr Campbell, a cattle salesman. During a hunting expedition with his cousins, he learned from Diana that he was charged with having committed a highway robbery, and she

escorted him to Squire Inglewood's, where he encountered his travelling companion as his accuser,
and was acquitted on the testimony of the Scotch
dealer. Having fallen in love with Diana, he discovered that she was destined for Rashleigh, or a
cloister, and that he was a hypocrite. During his
rival's absence from home, Frank gained his
cousin's confidence and became her constant companion. He also obtained important information
from Andrew Fairservice, and on returning from a
talk with him, witnessed an interview between his
lady-love and a male stranger. He next learnt
from her that Rashleigh was in charge of his
father's business while he was gone to Holland;
and, a few days later, she handed him a letter
announcing that his cousin had robbed the firm
and disappeared. Having advised his immediate
departure for Glasgow, she entrusted him with
another letter to be used under certain circumstances, and he started with Andrew as his servant.

In the cathedral there, some one whispered behind him, 'Meet me at midnight on the bridge,'
and, having done so, he was conducted to the
Tolbooth, and admitted by Dougal to a cell in
which he found Owen, who had been imprisoned
by MacVittie and MacFin. Presently his guide
hurried in, followed by Mr Jarvie, who was Mr
Osbaldistone's agent, and the stranger proved to
be Mr Campbell, *alias* Rob Roy, the bailie's
kinsman. The Highlander, to whom Diana's letter
was addressed, invited his relative and Frank to
dine with him at Aberfoil, and intimated that he
might be able to arrange Mr Osbaldistone's affairs.

Having been interrupted in a duel with Rashleigh, whom he met in the city, Frank started with Mr Jarvie and Andrew for the inn named by Campbell, where the bailie fought MacStuart with a red-hot poker, and they were arrested by Captain Thornton and his troops for being in communication with a proscribed robber. Dougal was also brought in as a spy, and accepted a bribe to betray Rob Roy's hiding-place. The red-coats, however, had scarcely disappeared with their prisoners, when the outlaw emerged from behind the inn with Rashleigh, upon a signal from whom he was seized by Galbraith and his troopers.

Captain Thornton and his party were led by their guide to a narrow pass, on entering which they were challenged by Roy's wife, and fired upon by a hidden force. In the scramble which ensued the bailie was suspended by his coat-tails to the branch of a tree, and they were surrounded by Highlanders. Mr Jarvie claimed relationship with his kinsman's spouse, but she scornfully ordered all the prisoners to be bound, and thrown into an adjacent lake. Suddenly her sons brought news of their father's capture, and, having denounced Rashleigh, she had despatched Frank with a message to the Duke of Argyle, when a shout echoed through the gorge, and Rob Roy rushed into his wife's arms. He had managed, with the connivance of one of the troopers, to set himself free as they crossed the river, and, by his expertness in swimming and diving, to escape pursuit. Frank was making his way back to the inn at Aberfoil, when he was overtaken by Diana

with an elderly escort, who bade her restore to her
cousin the papers Rashleigh had stolen from his
father, and they parted. Then he met MacGregor,
who accompanied him to the clachan, where they
found the bailie solacing himself for the rough
treatment he had undergone, and anxious to make
the outlaw's sons his apprentices.

On reaching Glasgow again Frank was welcomed
by his father, who had come thither with the intention of punishing his nephew; and, on their return
to London, he was allowed to join the army which
was being raised to put down the rebellion of
1715, in which Sir Hildebrand was taken prisoner
and died in Newgate, leaving Frank his heir. He
accordingly went to take possession of the estate;
and having learnt from Squire Inglewood that
the stranger who visited Diana was her father,
disguised as a priest, he was startled by their
sudden appearance in the library to claim his
protection as Papists. The next day Rashleigh
entered with them as prisoners; but they were
rescued by a party of Highlanders led by Mac-
Gregor, who plunged his sword into the traitor,
and the Vernons embarked for France. Mr
Osbaldistone was not a little shocked that his
son should entertain the idea of marrying a
Roman Catholic; but after some hesitation he
consented, under the belief that a dutiful daughter
could not but prove a good wife; and Rob Roy,
notwithstanding his many daring and perilous
adventures, died a peaceful death at a good old
age, remembered by his countrymen as the dread
of the wealthy, but the friend of the poor.

HEART OF MID-LOTHIAN

Principal Characters

CAPTAIN PORTEOUS, *an officer of the city guard.*
DAVID DEANS, *a dairy-farmer at St Leonard's Crags.*
JEANIE, } *his daughters.*
EFFIE,
THE LAIRD OF DUMBIEDYKES, *Jeanie's admirer.*
REUBEN BUTLER, *a schoolmaster, her real lover.*
MR BARTOLINI SADDLETREE, *Deans's cousin.*
SIR EDMUND STAUNTON, *Rector of Willingham.*
GEORGE STAUNTON, *alias* ROBERTSON, *his son.*
ANDREW WILSON, *a smuggler, his companion.*
MEG MURDOCKSON, *George's nurse.*

MADGE WILDFIRE, *her crazy daughter.*
SHARPITLAW, *a constable.*
JIM RATCLIFFE, *his subordinate.*
THE KING'S ADVOCATE.
MR FAIRBROTHER, *counsel for Effie.*
MRS BICKERTON, *landlady of the 'Seven Stars' at York.*
MRS GLASS, *a tobacconist.*
MACCALLUM MORE, DUKE OF ARGYLE.
MR ARCHIBALD, *his groom of the chamber.*
QUEEN CAROLINE, WIFE OF KING GEORGE II.
MRS DUTTON, *a dairywoman.*
DUNCAN KNOCK, *the Captain of Knockdunder.*
DONOCHA DHU, *a robber.*

Rioters, neighbours of the Deans, lords of justiciary, officers of the court and Tolbooth at Edinburgh, robbers, servants, etc.

Period, 1736. *Localities: Edinburgh, Midland Counties, London and Dumbartonshire.*

DURING the Porteous riots at Edinburgh, which arose from the escape of a convict named Robertson, and an attempt to rescue the body of his companion Wilson from the gallows, Effie Deans was arrested on suspicion of having murdered her newly-born child, and imprisoned in the Tolbooth. While Porteous was being dragged thence by the mob for execution, Robertson, disguised as a woman, urged her in vain to escape; and subsequently, meeting Butler, arranged an interview with Jeanie, to whom he confessed that he was Effie's lover, and explained how she might save her sister's life. Neither he, however, nor her father, nor even her sister's entreaties, could induce Jeanie to bear false witness at the trial. Effie's reply to the indictment was — 'Not guilty of my poor bairn's death;' but the verdict of the jury was against her, and she was condemned to be hanged. Jeanie at once determined to seek the queen's intercession for her sister; and having accepted a loan from Dumbiedykes, and obtained a letter from Butler to the Duke of Argyle, she started on foot for London.

Near Grantham her money was demanded by two ruffians, but on producing a pass which Ratcliffe had given her, they led the way to a barn, where she found Meg Murdockson and her daughter, and, during the night, overheard a conversation, from which she learnt that Robertson had deserted Madge for Effie. The next morning Jeanie gathered fuller particulars from Madge's rambling outbursts, and they came to Sir Edmund's church. Having parted with her crazed companion, Jeanie had an interview with the rector, and was then shown into a room, where Robertson proved to be his son. In a conversation which followed, George Staunton related all his misdeeds; and, having declined to tell her errand to his father, she proceeded on her journey, and reached London without any further adventure.

Having found her relation, Mrs Glass, Jeanie

obtained admission to the Duke of Argyle, to
whom she delivered Butler's letter, which contained a testimonial that an ancestor of his had
saved the life of his grace's grandfather, and he
promised that he would do his best for her. Two
days afterwards Mr Archibald came to escort her
to the duke, whose chariot was in waiting, and
with whom she travelled to the garden of the
royal lodge at Richmond, where she was allowed
to plead for her sister's pardon with Queen Caroline. In simple but pathetic sentences she appealed with such success that the queen assured
her she should not want her warm intercession
with His Majesty, and placed in her hand a
housewife, containing a bill for fifty pounds, as
a memento of their interview. She at once wrote
the joyful news to George Staunton, her father
and Butler; and then the duke called to tell
her that the pardon had been granted, with the
qualification that Effie should banish herself from
Scotland for fourteen years. He also arranged
that Jeanie should return under the care of Mr
Archibald and Mrs Dutton, and presented her
to his duchess and daughters. As the travellers
approached Carlisle a woman was being hanged
as a witch, and presently Madge Wildfire clung
to their carriage, entreating to be allowed to cut
down her mother. She was, however, seized and
ducked in a pool by the mob, and then carried
to the hospital, where Jeanie was with her when
she died.

In compliance with the duke's wish, instead of
going direct to Edinburgh, they proceeded to

Roseneath, where old Deans welcomed back his daughter, and she learnt that her sister had disappeared with Staunton. She was, however, consoled on hearing that his grace had engaged her father to superintend a farm in Dumbartonshire, and nominated Butler to the neighbouring kirk of Knocktarlitie. After an entertainment on the occasion of his ordination, as Jeanie lingered alone by the seashore, she was embraced by Effie, who had come with her lover to announce their marriage and say farewell. The minister's wedding soon followed; and five years afterwards came a letter from Lady Staunton, who was moving in the highest society in London, but in constant fear of the events of her early life transpiring. One day Mrs Butler, whose only unhappiness arose from the religious differences between her father and husband, discovered in her children's hands a broad-sheet containing the dying confession of Meg Murdockson, which strengthened her belief that her sister's child was living; and the same afternoon the Captain of Knockdunder brought her a visitor, who proved to be Effie. Sir George was on his way to the manse with Butler when he was shot in a skirmish by his son, who, Ratcliffe ascertained, had been sold to a ruffian named Donocha Dhu, and trained to a life of robbery and violence.

The secret was kept from his mother, who, after a while, sought solace for an aching heart by resuming her place in the world of fashion, and eventually died in the convent where she had received her post-nuptial education.

WAVERLEY

Principal Characters

SIR EVERARD WAVERLEY, *of Waverley Honour, a Tory.*
His brother, RICHARD, *a Whig.*
His sister, RACHEL.
His nephew, EDWARD, *an officer of English dragoons.*
MR PEMBROKE, *his tutor.*
HUMPHREY HOUGHTON,
DUGALD MAHONY,
JOHN HODGES,
ALICK POLWARTH, } *his soldier servants.*
COSMO COMYNE BRADWARDINE, *Baron of Tully-Veolan.*
His daughter, ROSE.
BAILIE MACWHEEBLE, *his steward.*
DAVID GELLATLEY, *his butler.*
His wife, JANET.
COLONEL GARDINER, *commander of Edward's regiment.*
MR FALCONER, *of Balmawhapple, a Whig laird.*
FERGUS MACIVOR, VICH IAN VOHR, *a Highland chieftain.*

His sister, FLORA.
CALLUM BEG, *his page.*
UNA,
CATHLEEN, } *Flora's attendants.*
EVAN DHU MACCOMBICH, *MacIvor's lieutenant.*
DONALD BEN LEAN, *a freebooter.*
His daughter, ALICE.
EBENEZER CRUICKSHANKS, *an innkeeper and guide.*
REV. MR MORTON, *a Presbyterian minister.*
MAJOR MELVILLE, *a justice of the peace.*
MR GILFILLAN, *a Cameronian leader.*
CHARLES EDWARD, THE YOUNG PRETENDER.
COLONEL TALBOT, *a friend of Sir Everard.*
LADY EMILY BLANDEVILLE, *his wife.*
RUTHVEN, *a pedlar.*

Highland clansmen, a blacksmith and his wife, English army, Highland army, a farmer and his family, clergymen, high sheriff, servants, etc.

Period, 1745. *Localities: Scotland and England.*

EDWARD WAVERLEY, who had been brought up as his uncle's heir, was on a visit to Bradwardine of Tully-Veolan and his daughter, when all their cows were driven off by armed Highlanders, in consequence of the baron having ceased paying blackmail to Vich Ian Vohr. During the day Evan Dhu arrived to compromise the matter, and invited Waverley to spend a few days with him in the mountains. Having made acquaintance with Ben Lean and Alice, he was met by the chieftain, who entertained him at his Highland mansion, and introduced him to his sister Flora. After spending three weeks most enjoyably in her society, he went with Fergus to a stag hunt, in which a large gathering of the clan took part, and, having been disabled by a severe sprain, he was left under the care of an old leech and Callum Beg, while the chieftain and his followers proceeded on a distant expedition. On returning to his host's house he found several letters awaiting him, and among them an order to join his regiment. In compliance, however, with his father's and uncle's desire, he resigned his commission, and then learnt from a newspaper that he was already superseded. This cleared the way for him to declare his love to Flora, who shared her brother's attachment to the Stuarts; but she advised him to seek a more suitable wife, and to serve the cause of his exiled sovereign among his own countrymen.

Next morning a letter from Rose informed him that the baron had joined the rising against the Hanoverian dynasty, and he started for Edinburgh, attended as far as a lowland village by Callum Beg, who secured him the services of Cruickshanks. On their way southwards he was seized as a Jacobite, and, at Mr Morton's suggestion,

taken before Major Melville, who handed him
over to Gilfillan to be lodged in Stirling Castle.
He was, however, rescued by two Highlanders,
and after being nursed through a fever by old
Janet, was escorted to the capital, where he was
introduced by Fergus to the Pretender, who accepted his allegiance, and girded him with the
sword he was wearing. At Holyrood he met
Flora and Rose; and, having joined the Highland
army, he distinguished himself at the battle of
Prestonpans, and saved the life of Colonel Talbot,
from whom he learnt that his father and uncle
were attainted of treason. He also ascertained
the circumstances under which he had incurred
the displeasure of Colonel Gardiner. Some weeks
afterwards he obtained a pass for Colonel Talbot,
who was his prisoner, to join his sick wife, and
Charles Edward resolved to advance into England. During the march the prince had to adjust
a quarrel between MacIvor and Waverley relating
to Rose; and at a council of war it was decided
to return northwards, on which Fergus declared
he should be dead or a captive before the morrow.
At sunset they encountered a troop of English
cavalry, and the chieftain was surrounded. Edward
escaped to a farmhouse, where he heard of his
father's death, and made his way to London.

Acting, however, on Colonel Talbot's advice, he
returned to Scotland just after the battle of Culloden; and, on reaching Tully-Veolan, he was led
by old Gellatley to a hut, where the baron was in
hiding with Janet, from whom he learnt how
greatly Rose had secretly helped him, and that

she was safe. He also heard that Fergus was
in Carlisle jail, and Flora with a lady there. In
a few days the colonel sent him protections for
himself and Bradwardine, upon which he at once
proposed for the baron's daughter, and was accepted. The next day they went to see her, and
Waverley's anxiety now was the fate of Vich Ian
Vohr and his foster brother Evan Dhu. He supplied money for their defence, but ere he reached
Carlisle they had been found guilty of treason.
At an interview with Flora she reproached herself
with having spurred her brother to his ruin, and
sent Rose a chain of diamonds as a wedding gift.
On the morning of the execution Waverley was
allowed to take leave of Fergus, who begged him
to befriend his clan, and bravely met his fate.
Sir Everard and his sister received their nephew
as a hero on his return to Waverley Honour, and
his marriage was celebrated as soon as the legal
settlements were completed. The baron was then
invited to accompany the bride and bridegroom to
his estate at Tully-Veolan, which he was led to
suppose had been purchased by Colonel Talbot;
but on arriving there he found that Waverley had
advanced the money to place him in full possession again, and had even succeeded in recovering
his ancestral drinking-cup, which had become the
spoil of King George's soldiers.

G

REDGAUNTLET

Principal Characters

MR DARSIE LATIMER, *after-wards* SIR ARTHUR DARSIE REDGAUNTLET.

MR SAUNDERS FAIRFORD, *a Writer to the Signet.*

His son, ALAN, *an advocate.*

MR HERRIES OF BIRRENS-WORK, *alias the* LAIRD OF REDGAUNTLET.

His niece, LILIAS.

CRISTAL NIXON, } *their ser-*
MABEL MOFFAT, } *vants.*

BENJIE, *a village laa.*

JOSHUA GEDDES, *of Mount Sharon, a Quaker tacksman.*

His sister, RACHEL.

WILLIE STEENSON, *a blind fiddler.*

PETER PEEBLES, *Alan's first client.*

MR WILLIAM CROSBIE, *Provost of Dumfries.*

SQUIRE FOXLEY, *of Foxley Hall Cumberland.*

MASTER NICHOLAS FAGGOT, *his clerk.*

MR PETER MAXWELL, *of Summertrees, alias* PATE-IN-PERIL.

TAM TRUMBULL, *of Annan, a contraband trader.*

NANTY EWART, *captain of the 'Jumping Jenny.'*

FATHER CRACKENTHORP, *a Cumberland innkeeper and smuggler.*

THE SISTERS ARTHURET, *of Fairladies' House.*

FATHER BUONAVENTURE, *after- .. 's* THE YOUNG PRETEN-DE!.

GENERAL CAMPBELL, *an Eng-lish officer.*

A fishers' merry-making, judges and advocates of Supreme Court at Edinburgh, armed fishermen, smugglers, guests at the inn, con-ference of Jacobite leaders, servants, etc.

Period, 1763. *Localities : Scotland and Cumberland.*

DARSIE had been Alan's favourite schoolfellow, and, to please his son, Mr Fairford had consented that the youth, who received an ample allowance on the understanding that he was to make no in-quiries respecting his family until he completed his

twenty-fifth year, should live with them. Alan
was studying for the law, but his companion had
started for his first country ramble, and the story
commences with a long correspondence between
them. As he returned from fishing in the Solway
Firth, with Benjie as his instructor, Darsie was
overtaken by the tide, and carried by Mr Herries,
dressed as a fisherman, on horseback to a cottage,
where Lilias said grace at supper-time; and next
morning he was placed under the guidance of
Joshua Geddes. The Quaker, who was part owner
of some fishing nets in the river, invited him to
spend a few days at his house; and while there
he heard from Alan that a young lady had called
to warn him that his friend was in considerable
danger, and to urge that he should at once return
to Edinburgh. A letter, however, from old Fairford determined him not to do so; and having made
acquaintance with the blind fiddler, who told him
a tale of the Redgauntlet family, Darsie went with
him to a fishers' merry-making, where he danced
with Lilias, who reproached him for leading an
idle life, and begged him to leave the neighbourhood.

Mr Fairford had arranged that Peter Peebles, an
eccentric suitor, should be his son's first client, and
he was pleading the cause before the Lords Ordin-
ary when his father, by mistake, handed him a
letter from Mr Crosbie, announcing that Darsie
had mysteriously disappeared. Alan instantly
rushed out of court, and started in search of his
friend, who had accompanied the Quaker to await
an attack on his fishing station, and been made

prisoner by the rioters, of whom Mr Herries was
the leader. After being nearly drowned, and recovering from a fever, he awoke in a strange
room, to which he was confined for several days,
when he was visited by his captor, and conducted
by him to an interview with Squire Foxley, who,
acting as a magistrate, declined to interfere with
Mr Herries' guardianship. As the squire was leaving, however, Mr Peebles arrived to apply for a
warrant against Alan for throwing up his brief,
and startled Mr Herries by recognising him as a
Redgauntlet and an unpardoned Jacobite. Darsie
obtained a partial explanation from him, and was
told to prepare for a journey disguised as a woman.
Meanwhile, Alan had applied to the provost, and,
having obtained from his wife's relation, Mr Maxwell, a letter to Herries, he started for Annan,
where, under the guidance of Trumbull, he took
ship for Cumberland. On landing at Craken-
thorp's inn, he was transported by Nanty Ewart,
and a gang of smugglers, to Fair-ladies' House,
where he was nursed through a fever, and introduced to Father Buonaventure. After being closely
questioned and detained for a few days, he was
allowed to return with a guide to the inn.

Darsie was also travelling thither with Herries
and his followers, when he discovered that Lilias,
who accompanied them, was his sister, and learnt
from her his own real name and rank. He was
also urged by his uncle to join a rising in favour
of the Pretender; and, having hesitated to do so,
was detained in custody when they reached their
destination, where Alan, as well as other visitors

and several of the neighbouring gentry, had already arrived. He was then introduced to a conference of Charles Edward's adherents, and afterwards to the prince himself, who refused to agree to their conditions, and decided to abandon the contemplated attempt in his favour. Ewart was, accordingly, ordered to have his brig in readiness, when Nixon suggested that he should turn traitor, upon which they fought and killed each other. Sir Arthur now learned that Fairford and Geddes were in the house ; but, before he was allowed to see them, they had been shown into the room where Lilias was waiting, when Alan became aware that his fair visitor at Edinburgh was his friend's sister, and heard from her lips all the particulars of her brother's history. Their conversation was interrupted by the entrance of Benjie, in whose pocket a paper was found indicating that Nixon had communicated with the Government ; and, during the confusion which ensued, General Campbell arrived, and announced that he was sufficiently supported with cavalry and infantry. His instructions, however, from King George were to allow all concerned in the plot to disperse, and he intimated that as many as wished might embark in the vessel which was in waiting.

The Pretender was, accordingly, led by the Laird of Redgauntlet to the beach, and Lilias offered to accompany her uncle in his voluntary exile. This, however, he would not permit, and, after an exchange of courtesies with the general, the prince departed amidst the tears and sobs of the last supporters of his cause, and henceforward the term Jacobite ceased to be a party name. Lilias, of course, married Alan, and Herries, who had asked his nephew's pardon for attempting to make a rebel of him, threw away his sword, and became the prior of a monastery.

GUY MANNERING

Principal Characters

MR GUY MANNERING, *afterwards a colonel in the Indian army.*
MRS MANNERING, *his wife.*
Their daughter, JULIA.
LIEUTENANT ARCHER, *a favourite of Mrs Mannering.*
MR GODFREY BERTRAM, *of Ellangowan.*
His sister, MARGARET BERTRAM.
His son, HARRY, *alias* VANBEEST BROWN.
His daughter, LUCY.
MR CHARLES HAZLEWOOD, *her lover.*
DOMINIE SAMPSON, *a village schoolmaster, and afterwards Harry's tutor.*
MEG MERRILIES, *a gipsy.*
GILBERT GLOSSIN, *an attorney.*
SCROW, *his clerk.*

DIRK HATTERAICK, *a Dutch smuggler.*
MR FRANK KENNEDY, *a supervisor of Excise.*
MR MACMORLAN, *Sheriff-Substitute of Dumfries.*
MRS MACMORLAN, *his wife.*
MR AND MRS MERVYN, *friends of Colonel Mannering.*
DANDIE DINMONT, *a farmer.*
MRS MACCANDLISH, *hostess of 'The Gordon Arms' at Kippletringan.*
DEACON BEARSCLIFF, *a villager.*
BROWN, *a smuggler.*
TIB MUMPS, *mistress of a public-house.*
MACGUFFOG, *a constable.*
TOD GABRIEL, *a fox-hunter.*
MR PAULUS PLEYDELL, *an advocate from Edinburgh.*

Smugglers, constables, soldiers and villagers.

Period, 1765. *Localities: Scotland, Cumberland, Holland and India.*

GUY MANNERING, after leaving Oxford, had been Mr Godfrey Bertram's guest on the night of his son's birth, when he made acquaintance with Dominie Sampson, and with Meg Merrilies, who came to tell the infant's fortune. The young student, however, offered to do this from the stars, and predicted that three periods of the boy's life

would be very hazardous. Five years afterwards
he was kidnapped while riding with Kennedy,
whose dead body was found on the beach; and
the same night, after giving birth to a daughter,
Mrs Bertram left her husband a widower.

Sixteen more years had elapsed when Colonel
Mannering returned from India just in time to be
present at his friend's death, and Glossin, who had
been concerned in Harry's abduction, became the
possessor of the Ellangowan estate. Lucy and the
dominie accepted the hospitality of Mr and Mrs
MacMorlan; but the colonel, having learnt from
Mr Mervyn, at whose house his daughter was
staying, that she had a lover, who afterwards
proved to be Brown, hired a house in the neighbourhood of Kippletringan, and invited Miss Bertram to be Julia's companion, and the tutor his
librarian.

As he was following Miss Mannering to Scotland, Brown, whom the colonel believed he had
shot in a duel in India, dined with Dinmont at an
inn, where he also met Meg Merrilies, who recognised him; and, having rescued the farmer from
some robbers, he spent a few days at his house.
Proceeding on his journey, he came to a ruined
hut, in which the gipsy was tending a dying man;
and, hidden by her, he saw a gang of ruffians
divide the contents of his portmanteau, and bury
their comrade. When they had gone she pointed
out his road, and gave him a purse, exacting at
the same time a promise that he would come with
her whenever she called for him.

Writing to a friend, Julia made great fun of the

dominie's peculiarities, and mentioned Lucy's discouragement of young Hazlewood because she had no fortune. In her next letter she described an attack upon their house at Woodbourne by smugglers; and in another the sudden appearance of Brown, who had wounded Hazlewood and escaped. Glossin, now a justice of the peace, was indefatigable in endeavouring to trace him, and heard with pleasure that MacGuffog had a man in custody. He, however, was Hatteraick, in whose smuggling ventures the attorney had largely shared, and who told him that Harry Bertram was in the neighbourhood. Having connived at his escape from custody, Glossin met him in a cave, and learnt that the young heir had been carried to Holland, where he was adopted by a merchant named Vanbeest, who afterwards sent him to India. The attorney then called at Woodbourne to announce that Miss Bertram had left her fortune to Lucy, and the colonel at once started with the dominie to Edinburgh, to place the matter in Mr Pleydell's hands.

Harry had retreated to Cumberland, but he managed to correspond with Julia; and, having returned to Ellangowan, he was wandering among the ruins when he encountered Glossin, who had him arrested for shooting at Hazlewood, and lodged in the bridewell adjoining the custom-house at Portanferry. Here he was visited by Dinmont, who had heard from Gabriel of his being in trouble, and was allowed to pass the night with him. Meanwhile Meg Merrilies had sent a paper to the colonel by the dominie, and urged young

Hazlewood to cause the soldiers who had been withdrawn from Portanferry to be sent back there instantly. During the night the custom-house was fired by a gang of ruffians; but one of them helped Bertram and his friend to escape, and led them to a carriage, which conveyed them to Woodbourne, where Mr Pleydell had previously arrived. Having been recognised by the colonel as Brown, and questioned by the lawyer, his identity as the heir of Ellangowan was established, and he was hugged by the dominie as 'his little Harry.' The next morning Lucy embraced her long-lost brother, and Julia acknowledged him as her lover.

As he was walking with them, Meg Merrilies sent Dinmont to claim Bertram's compliance with his promise to her; and, followed also by Hazlewood, she led the way to a room where she armed them, and thence to the smugglers' cave, where, after a struggle, in which the gipsy was mortally wounded, they seized Hatteraick and handed him over to the village constables. Meg's dying revelations furnished sufficient evidence for arresting Glossin, who, by bribing the jailer, obtained access to the smuggler's cell, where he was found strangled, and his accomplice in crime committed suicide. Having recovered the property of his ancestors, Harry Bertram was able to discharge all his father's debts, and, with the help of Julia's dowry, to erect a new mansion, which contained a snug chamber called 'Mr Sampson's apartment.' His aunt's estate also reverted to him, but he resigned it to his sister on her marriage with Hazlewood.

THE HIGHLAND WIDOW

Principal Characters

HAMISH MACTAVISH MOHR, *an outlaw.*
ELSPAT, *his wife.*
HAMISH BEAN, *their son.*
MILES PHADRAICK, *a farmer.*

REV. MICHAEL TYRIE, *a Presbyterian minister.*
GREEN COLIN, *captain of Hamish Bean's regiment.*
ALLAN BREAK CAMERON, *his sergeant.*

Private soldiers, Highland women, a regimental parade.

Period, 1775. *Locality : Scotland, near Oban.*

HAMISH MOHR, a daring freebooter, had met his death in an encounter with the Saxon red-coats, by whom the Highlands were garrisoned after the battle of Culloden. His wife, who had shared all his dangers, strove to inspire their only son with his father's love of adventure and hatred of servile toil; but as he grew up the lad evinced no inclination for lawless pursuits, and, unable to endure his mother's taunts at his want of spirit, enlisted in one of the regiments formed in Scotland to oppose the French in the American war of independence. Before sailing he sent her some money by Phadraick, and returned to spend a few days with her, when she fiercely reproached him for daring to act in opposition to her will, and, failing to alter his purpose, drugged his parting-cup, thus causing him to exceed his furlough, and render himself liable to the lash as a deserter. She then urged him to flee to her kinsmen, while she baffled his pursuers ; but he resolved to await the arrival of the sergeant and men of his regiment who, he felt sure, would be sent to arrest him. They came, and, on being summoned to surrender, he shot the sergeant dead. The other soldiers secured him, and he was marched as a prisoner to Dumbarton castle, where he was tried by court-martial and condemned to be shot. His captain and a Presbyterian minister interceded for him ; but the English general in command was determined to make an example, and the next morning his sentence was carried out in the presence of his comrades.

His mother, who had attempted to follow him, was met by the minister wandering in a wild glen, and on hearing her son's fate, she uttered terrible imprecations, and renounced all further intercourse with the world. She lived, however, for many years in her lonely cottage, regarded with awe and pity by her neighbours as the victim of destiny, rather than the voluntary cause of her son's death and her own wretchedness. At length, while two women, who had been set to watch her last moments, were sleeping, she disappeared from her bed, and was never heard of again.

THE SURGEON'S DAUGHTER

Principal Characters

MR GIDEON GRAY, of Middle-
mas, a village surgeon.
His wife, JEAN.
Their daughter, MENIE.
MR RICHARD TRESHAM, *after-
wards* GENERAL WITHER-
INGTON.
MDLLE. ZILIA DE MONÇADA,
afterwards his wife.
Their son, RICHARD.
MATHIAS DE MONÇADA, *a
Portuguese Jew.*
MR LAWFORD, *Town Clerk of
Middlemas.*
TOM HILLARY, *his apprentice.*

ADAM HARTLEY, *Mr Gray's
apprentice.*
MR M'FITTOCH, *a dancing
master.*
CAPTAIN SEELENCOOPER, *Gov-
ernor of Military Hospital at
Ryde.*
BARAK EL HADJI, *an agent of
Hyder Ali.*
MADAME DE MONTREVILLE, *a
Begum.*
PAUPIAH, *steward to the British
resident.*
HYDER ALI, *Rajah of Mysore.*
TIPPOO SAIB, *his son.*

*Village nurses, king's messenger, servants, English residents at
Madras, natives, courtiers and officers of Tippoo Saib's household, retinue of the Begum.*

Period, 1780. *Localities : Fifeshire, Isle of Wight and India.*

THE surgeon's services were unexpectedly sought
by Richard's parents, who arrived in the village,
as strangers, just before his birth. The following
day the father left, and within a month the mother
was carried off by her father, who persuaded Mr
Gray to undertake the care and education of the
boy, and deposited a thousand pounds in trust
for him. Four years afterwards Mrs Gray died
in giving birth to a daughter, and the two children
were brought up together. At the age of fourteen

Richard, who had been led by his nurse to believe himself born to wealth and honour, was informed by his guardian of his real position, and, after consulting with Mr Lawford and his companion Hillary, he decided to remain an inmate of Mr Gray's family as his apprentice, with Hartley as a fellow pupil. As they grew up both the young men fell in love with Menie, and when the doctor proposed that Hartley should become his partner, and endeavour to secure her affections, it transpired that she and Richard were already secretly engaged. Hartley determined to make a voyage to India, and learnt with astonishment that his rival, at the instigation of Hillary, who was now a captain in the Company's service, intended to spend two years there before marrying, in the hope of realising a fortune.

Having obtained the money left by his grandfather in Mr Gray's hands, and enlisted as a recruit, he sailed from Edinburgh with his friend for the depot at Ryde; but, on recovering from a drinking bout before landing, he found himself in the military hospital, deserted by Hillary, and robbed of all his belongings. Hartley, however, was acting as one of the medical officers, and, having earned the gratitude of the commandant, General Witherington, by successfully treating two of his children who were suffering from small-pox, was able to obtain a commission for his fellow-student. The general and his wife had discovered that Richard was their first-born, and when he was introduced to them the shock of hearing him describe himself as an orphan, deserted by his

parents, caused the death of his mother, upon
which the father was seized with a fit of frenzy,
and on recovering could not face his son again.
Hartley had, however, been previously entrusted
with his history, as well as a gift of money for
him, and they sailed together for Madras. Having killed his colonel in a duel, Richard fled
to the court of a native prince, while Hartley
obtained great reputation as a medical prac-
titioner. One of his patients was Barak el Hadji,
who promised him his influence with Hyder Ali,
should he at any time need it.

Some months afterwards he was startled by the
presence of Menie Gray at a public breakfast,
chaperoned by the Begum, who, he learnt, was
the wealthy widow of a Rajah. At a private
interview with his old master's daughter, Hartley
elicited from her that she had come out at
Richard's invitation to be married, and was on
her way to meet him in Mysore. Mistrusting
her lover, he offered his protection should she
need it, and the next day he received a note
from her telling him she was sold to Tippoo Saib.
Unable to obtain an audience of the governor,
Hartley resolved to solicit the intervention of
Hyder Ali, and, having reached Seringapatam,
he sought the aid of El Hadji, who introduced
him to another Fakir of higher rank. Following
his directions, he accompanied a troop of native
cavalry to Tippoo's encampment near Bangalore,
and witnessed his return thither, escorted by a
magnificent bodyguard, including artillery and
elephants. The Begum, who had previously

arrived with her retinue, and Menie under her
protection, was at once invited to an interview
with the prince in his garden the following day.
Accordingly at noon the discharge of cannon
announced that he had left his palace ; and on
the arrival of his visitor, attended by Richard
as her principal officer, she was conducted to a
cushion on his right hand. An attendant then
proclaimed the appointment of Richard as governor of the city, and the Begum in return presented Tippoo with the litter containing Menie.

The old Fakir, however, came forward, and,
throwing off his disguise, ascended the throne as
Hyder Ali. Having reproved his son, he commanded him to restore the gift to the care of
Hartley, but allowed the ceremony of investiture
to proceed. As Richard, however, who had
plotted with Paupiah to betray his trust, was
about to mount the elephant in waiting for him,
the Rajah made a sign, upon which the animal
seized him by the neck with its trunk, and crushed
him to death with its foot. The Begum was then
ordered to bear her share in compensating her
intended victim for the indignity she had suffered,
and afterwards deprived of her power and riches.
Menie returned to her native village, and the
gallant Hartley died from a distemper caught in
the courageous pursuit of his profession.

THE TAPESTRIED CHAMBER

Principal Characters

GENERAL BROWNE, *returned from the American war.*
THE LANDLORD *of an inn.*

LORD WOODVILLE, *of Woodville Castle.*
THE APPARITION OF A WOMAN.

Visitors at the castle, servants.

Period, 1782. *Locality: the west of England.*

THIS is a ghost story. While travelling through the western counties, the general's attention was attracted by a picturesquely situated old castle, and, on inquiry at the inn where he changed horses, he learnt that its owner was a nobleman who had been his schoolfellow. He accordingly determined to call upon his lordship; and, having been persuaded to be his guest for a week, he was conducted at bedtime to an old-fashioned room, hung with tapestry, but comfortably furnished, and well lighted by two large candles and a blazing fire. The next morning Lord Woodville was informed by his servant that the general had been wandering in the park since an early hour and when he appeared at the breakfast table his countenance was haggard, his clothes carelessly put on, and his manner abstracted; moreover, he announced that he must depart immediately. Drawing him aside from the other visitors, his

H

host pressed him for an explanation, and, after declaring that he would rather face a battery than recall the events of the night, he reluctantly narrated what he had undergone.

Just as he was falling asleep he heard the rustling of a silk gown, and the tapping of high-heeled shoes, and then the figure of a woman passed between the bedstead and the fireplace. At first her back was towards him, but she slowly turned, and he distinctly saw the features of a corpse, bearing traces of the most hideous passions. He started up, and she sat on the bed, advancing her face within half a yard of his, upon which all his courage forsook him and he swooned. On recovering his senses she had disappeared, but he was afraid to move until daybreak, when he hurried from the room thoroughly unnerved. Lord Woodville was deeply impressed, for the chamber had the reputation of being haunted; and as he conducted the general through his picture gallery, he suddenly started as he caught sight of a portrait, exclaiming, 'There she is!' and it proved to be the likeness of an ancestress whose crimes, he was told, had been too horrible for recital.

THE TWO DROVERS

Principal Characters

ROBIN OIG MACCOMBICH, *a Highland drover*.
JANET OF TOMAHOURICH, *his aunt*.
HUGH MORRISON OF GLANAE, *a Lowland drover*.
HARRY WAKEFIELD, *an English drover*.

MR IREBY, *a Cumberland squire*.
JOHN FLEECEBUMPKIN, *his bailiff*.
RALPH HESKETT, *host of an alehouse*.
DAME HESKETT, *his wife*.

Company at the alehouse, constables, judge and jury at Carlisle.

Period, 1795. *Localities: Perthshire and Cumberland.*

ROBIN OIG was just starting from Doune with a drove of cattle for England, when his father's sister, who was supposed to be gifted with second sight, drew his dirk from the folds of his plaid, and, exclaiming that there was Saxon blood on it, induced him to entrust the weapon to Morrison, who undertook to return it when asked for. At Falkirk the Highlander met his bosom friend, Wakefield, and they travelled southwards together. Having reached Cumberland, they separated to hire pasturage for their beasts, and it happened that while the Englishman bargained with the bailiff, the Highlander came to terms with the squire, and they thus both secured the same enclosure. On discovering this, Wakefield

115

reproached his comrade with having played him
false, and, angrily refusing his offer that they
should share the field, had to be content with a
barren moor belonging to the landlord of the alehouse, where they had agreed to pass the night.

The squire had invited Oig to sup with him,
and mentioned having passed Morrison a few miles
off. On reaching the inn the Highlander met
with a cold reception from the assembled company, who sided with Wakefield, and egged him
on to challenge Oig to a Cumberland tussle. But
the Highlander would have shaken hands, and,
refusing to fight except with swords, he attempted
to leave the room. Wakefield, however, opposed
his doing so, and struck him senseless to the
ground. Frantic with rage when he revived, and
prevented by the hostess from attacking his comrade, Oig sullenly went out, warning him to
beware. Striding over the moonlit moor to meet
Morrison, he obtained his dirk on the pretence
that he had enlisted, and, returning to the alehouse, he stabbed Wakefield through the heart.

At his trial the judge made every allowance for
the provocation Oig had received, but pointed out
to the jury that, as he went to recover possession
of his weapon, there was ample time for his passion
to have subsided, and for him to have reflected
on the guilt of his meditated revenge. He was,
accordingly, convicted of murder, and having been
sentenced to be hung, he met his fate with the
observation, 'I give a life for the life I took, and
what can I do more?'

THE ANTIQUARY

Principal Characters

MR WILLIAM LOVELL, *afterwards* LORD GERALDIN.
MRS MACLEUCHAR, *proprietress of the Queensferry diligence.*
MR JONATHAN OLDBUCK, *of Monkbarns, an Antiquary.*
MISS GRISELDA OLDBUCK, *his sister.*
CAPTAIN HECTOR MACINTYRE, *their nephew.*
MISS MARIA MACINTYRE, *their niece.*
CAXON, *a barber.*
His daughter, JENNY.
LIEUTENANT TAFFRIL, *her lover.*
EDIE OCHILTREE, *a mendicant.*
SIR ARTHUR WARDOUR, *of Knockwinnock Castle.*
His son, CAPTAIN REGINALD WARDOUR.

His daughter, ISABELLA.
HERMAN DOUSTERSWIVEL, *a charlatan professor.*
MRS MAILSETTER, *postmistress of Fairport.*
REV. DOCTOR BLATTERGOWL, *minister of Trotcosey.*
MISS REBECCA BLATTERGOWL, *his sister.*
ELSPETH, *of the Craigburnfoot.*
SAUNDERS MUCKLEBACKIT, *her son, a fisherman.*
THE COUNTESS OF GLENALLAN.
THE EARL, *her son.*
EVELINE NEVILLE, *his betrothed.*
BAILIE LITTLEJOHN.
MESSRS GREENHORN & GRINDERSON, *Writers to the Signet*

Servants, neighbours, fishermen, funeral procession, foresters, bowl-players, constables, bailiffs, etc.

Period, 1795. *Locality: Fifeshire.*

MR OLDBUCK, having made acquaintance with Lovell as they travelled together from Edinburgh to Fairport, invited him to Monkbarns, and finding him an intelligent listener to his antiquarian talk, introduced him to Sir Arthur and to Miss Isabella, with whom he had fallen in love in Yorkshire. On their way home from

meeting him at dinner, the baronet and his
daughter were overtaken by the tide, and Lovell,
with Ochiltree's help, rescued them from a ledge
of rock. Passing the night in a haunted room
at Monkbarns, he dreamt that he saw an old
burgomaster emerge from the tapestry, and point
to a motto in a book meaning that 'skill wins
favour.' When he called, however, the next day
at the castle, Miss Wardour declined his ad-
dresses, and he learnt from Mr Oldbuck that her
father was being swindled by Dousterswivel. A
letter he received caused him to seclude himself
in his lodgings for a fortnight, when he accepted
an invitation from Sir Arthur to a picnic at St
Ruth's Priory, where he was called upon to read
a legend transcribed by his lady-love, and challenged by MacIntyre for passing under an assumed
name.

Having wounded the captain, he was carried off
by the mendicant to a gallery in the ruins until he
could take refuge on board Lieutenant Taffril's
brig; and from their hiding-place they witnessed
an interview between the baronet and the professor, during which the latter pretended to un-
earth a ram's horn filled with coins. Believing
that more treasure was concealed in the ruins,
Sir Arthur, who had already borrowed largely
from his friend, came to ask for another hundred
pounds, which Dousterswivel demanded for con-
tinuing the search; but the antiquary insisted
that they should hire diggers and proceed at once
to the spot, where they were joined by Ochiltree,
and in an old grave found a chest containing

several ingots of silver, which had been secretly
placed there by Lovell's direction. The same
night, as the professor, accompanied by the mendicant, was digging in the hope of finding another
chest, he received a violent blow from a dark
figure, and fell insensible into the hole.

On recovering, he was startled by witnessing the
funeral service of the Countess of Glenallan in the
transept by torchlight, and was assisted to the
forester's lodge vowing vengeance for the trick
that had been played him. Shortly afterwards
Mucklebackit's son Steenie reached the fisherman's cottage, followed by Ochiltree, and produced the professor's pocket-book from his pouch.
The next morning old Elspeth sent the beggar
to tell the Earl of Glenallan she must see him
instantly, and, while he was settling a dispute
among the village bowl-players on his return, the
news arrived that Steenie was drowned, and he
was arrested on a charge of robbing and assault-
ing Dousterswivel.

As Hector was accompanying his uncle to the
lad's funeral, he was thrown down by a seal, and
to escape his raillery returned home. Mr Oldbuck, however, proceeded, and won the respect of
all the mourners by heading the procession to the
grave. The same afternoon the earl had an interview with Elspeth, and learnt from her that, having
married Eveline against his mother's wish, he had
been falsely told by her that she was his sister,
which had caused the poor girl to throw herself
from a cliff, and had for twenty years overwhelmed
him with grief and horror. The old woman also

led him to hope that his infant son was still
living. Meeting the antiquary, he opened his
heart to him, notwithstanding he had been a
rival for Eveline's hand, and at once received
the promise of his help in clearing up the
mystery.

Meanwhile Sir Arthur was on the point of leaving Knockwinnock Castle in possession of his
creditors, when Ochiltree, who had been bailed
by Mr Oldbuck, brought a letter from his son
Reginald enclosing funds and a bill of suspension.
The same night old Caxon having mistaken a
bonfire of the professor's laboratory for a beacon-
signal that the French were coming, the yeomanry
and volunteers were called out, and a Major
Neville arrived to take command of them. The
magistrates received him, and to their surprise
recognised their late visitor Lovell, who had disappeared after his duel with MacIntyre. The
antiquary took an opportunity of questioning him
privately, and, satisfied as to his identity, presented
him to the Earl of Glenallan as his son and heir.
Miss Wardour made no objection to become Lady
Geraldin, the old mendicant passed most of his
time with the barber, whose daughter was married
to the lieutenant, and Mr Oldbuck was always a
welcome visitor both at Knockwinnock and Glenallan House.

ST RONAN'S WELL

Principal Characters

MEG DODS, *hostess of the Cleikum Inn.*

VALENTINE BULMER, *afterwards* EARL OF ETHRINGTON.

FRANCIS TYRREL, *his half-brother.*

MASTER BINDLOOSE, *sheriff's clerk and banker.*

MR JOHN MOWBRAY *of Shaw's Castle, laird of St Ronan's.*

His sister, CLARA.

HANNAH IRWIN, *their cousin.*

NELLY TROTTER, *a fish-woman.*

LADY PENELOPE PENFEATHER.

MRS MARGARET BLOWER, *a widow.*

MISS MARIA DIGGES.

SIR BINGO BINKS, *an English baronet.*

MISS RACHEL BONNYRIGG, *afterwards* LADY BINKS.

DR QUACKLEBEN,
MR PHILIP WINTERBLOSSOM,
MR SAUNDERS MEIKLEHAM,
CAPTAIN HECTOR MACTURK,
REV. SIMON CHATTERLY,
MR MICHAEL MEREDITH,
MR PEREGRINE TOUCHWOOD. } *Managing Committee at St Ronan's Spa.*

SCROGIE

REV. JOSIAH CARGILL, *minister of St Ronan's.*

CAPTAIN JEKYL, *the earl's friend.*

SOLMES, *the earl's valet.*

Company at the Fox hotel, visitors at St Ronan's Spa, servants, etc.

Period, 1812. *Locality: near the Firth of Forth.*

BULMER and Tyrrel had been Mrs Dod's guests as students from Edinburgh, and she gladly welcomed Francis when he arrived, some years afterwards, to stay at the inn again, that he might fish and sketch in the neighbourhood. A mineral spring had, in the meantime, been discovered at St Ronan's, and he was invited by the fashionable visitors to dine

with them at the Fox Hotel, where he quarrelled
with Sir Bingo, and, on his way back to the
Cleikum, met Clara Mowbray, to whom he had
been secretly engaged during his former visit, but
was prevented from marrying her by the treachery
of Bulmer, who had now succeeded to the earldom,
and was expected at the Spa.   Tyrrel having been
waited upon by Captain MacTurk, accepted a
challenge from the baronet, but failed to keep his
appointment, and was posted as an adventurer by
the committee of management.   He also disappeared from the inn, which led his hostess to
consult Mr Bindloose, under the belief that he
had been murdered.   Their conference was interrupted by Mr Touchwood, who came to change a
bill, and talked of having been abroad for many
years.   He also evinced great interest in the affairs
of the Mowbray family, and having taken up his
quarters at the Cleikum, made friends with Mr
Cargill, who had been disappointed in love, and
startled him with a rumour that Clara was about
to be married.

Soon after the earl's arrival it was reported that
he had been shot in the arm by a foot-pad; and,
while his wound was healing, he spent his time in
gambling with the young laird of St Ronan's, who
had borrowed his sister's money for the purpose of
retrieving his luck.   Having allowed him to win a
considerable sum, his lordship made proposals for
Clara's hand, explaining that his grand-uncle had
disinherited his only son, and devised his estate to
him, on condition that he chose as a wife a lady of
the name of Mowbray.   In a letter to his friend

Jekyl, the earl confessed that he had been winged in a duel with Tyrrel, whom he met on his way to fight Sir Bingo, and that he had wounded his brother. A few days afterwards the company at the Well assembled at Shaw's Castle to take part in a dramatic entertainment, and Mr Touchwood persuaded Mr Cargill to accompany him as one of the guests. While they were walking in the grounds the minister took an opportunity to remind Clara of a secret in his keeping, which made it impossible for her to marry. He also encountered the earl, and, believing him to be Bulmer, attempted to warn him.

The next morning, as Mowbray was endeavouring to induce Clara to consent to the match, he received an anonymous communication that the earl was an impostor; and, in an interview with him, she rejected his suit with loathing and scorn. His lordship then wrote to Jekyl, telling him the circumstances under which, when he was only sixteen, he had arranged with Mr Cargill for a secret marriage between her and Tyrrel; but, learning subsequently the contents of his uncle's will, had incurred their life-long hatred by personating his brother at the ceremony. Tyrrel, who after the duel had retired to an adjacent village to be cured of his wound, reappeared just in time to rescue Mr Touchwood from drowning; and, at an interview with Jekyl, who undertook to clear his character, offered to forego his claim to the earldom, of which he had proofs, if his brother would refrain from molesting Clara any further. This proposal the earl sneered at, and, as he was forming fresh

schemes for attaining his end, he discovered that
Hannah Irwin, who had been Clara's companion,
was dying at St Ronan's, and anxious to confess
her share in the secret marriage. Solmes was
instructed to carry her off, while his master got
the brother into his power by ruining him at play,
and then promised to cancel the debt if Clara
consented to acknowledge him as her husband
within four-and-twenty hours.

Mowbray believed he had prevailed with his
sister, when Mr Touchwood unexpectedly arrived,
and announced himself as Scrogie, the disinherited
son, who by bribing Solmes, and in other ways,
had learnt everyone's secrets, and was ready with
his fortune to arrange all their difficulties. But he
was too late. Clara had escaped from her room
during the night, and, after appearing at the manse
to forgive her cousin, who had been confided to
Mr Cargill's care, had made her way to the Cleikum,
where, in a seeming trance, she had a final interview with Tyrrel, and died soon afterwards from
congestion of the brain. Mowbray, meanwhile, in
his search for her, encountered the earl and his
companions engaged in a shooting match, and
killed him in a duel arranged on the spot by
Captain MacTurk, with whom he fled to the Continent to escape imprisonment. Mr Touchwood
had consequently to seek some other outlet for his
wealth, and the Etherington estates were never
claimed by the rightful heir, who determined to
pass the remainder of his life in a Moravian
mission.

INDEX OF THE
PRINCIPAL CHARACTERS

	PAGE		PAGE
A BENEDICTINE ABBESS,	5	Archibald, Mr,	90
Advocate, The King's,	90	Argyle, Duke of,	90
Agatha (a servant),	1	Argyle, Marquis of,	54
Agelastes, Michael,	1	Armstrong, Grace,	82
Alasco, Doctor,	43	Armstrong, John,	48
Albany, Duke of,	22	Arthuret, The Sisters,	98
Aldrovand, Father,	5	Ashton, Henry,	71
Alexius Comnenus,	1	Ashton, Lady,	71
Alice Ben Lean,	94	Ashton, Lucy,	71
Alice Bridgenorth,	62	Ashton, Sholto Douglas	71
Alice Lee,	58	Ashton, Sir William,	71
Alice, of Ravenswood,	71	Astarte (an attendant),	1
Altramont, Frederick,	75	Athelstane (a Saxon),	14
Ambrose, Father,	39	Augusta of Berkely, Lady,	18
Amelot (a page),	5	Austria, Leopold, Arch-	
Amy Robsart,	43	duke of,	9
Anderson (a servant),	54	Auxerre, Bishop of,	27
Anjou, Margaret of,	31	Avenel, Julian,	35
Anna, Princess,	1	Avenel, Mary,	35
Annaple, Dame,	82	Avenel, White Lady of,	35
Anne of Geierstein,	31	Avenel, Widow Alice,	35
Annot Lyle,	54	Aymer, Prior of,	12
Anselm, Prior,	22		
Antioch, Bohemond of,	1		
Antonio (a guide),	31	BALDERSTON, Caleb,	71
Apparition of a Woman,	113	Balderston, Mysie,	71
Archer, Lieutenant,	103	Baldringham, Lady of	5

	PAGE
Baldwin, Archbishop, .	5
Baldwin, Count, . .	1
Balfour of Burley, John, .	67
Balmawhapple, Mr Falconer of, . . .	94
Barak El Hadji, . .	109
Bearscliff, Deacon, . .	103
Beaujeau, Princess of France, . . .	27
Beaujeu (a tavern-keeper),	50
Beaumanoir, Lucas de, .	14
Beg, Callum (a page), .	94
Bellenden, Edith, . .	67
Bellenden, Lady Margaret of, ...	67
Bellenden, Major, . .	67
Belue, Cardinal John of, .	27
Benjie (a village lad), .	98
Ben Lean, Alice, . .	94
Ben Lean, Donald, . .	94
Berengaria, Queen, . .	9
Berenger, Eveline, . .	5
Berenger, Sir Raymond de,	5
Berkely, Lady Augusta of,	16
Bertha (a servant), . .	1
Bertram (a minstrel), .	18
Bertram, Augustine, .	18
Bertram, Harry, . .	103
Bertram, Lucy, . .	103
Bertram, Miss Margaret, .	103
Bertram, Mr Godfrey, .	103
Berwine (a servant), .	5
Bevis (a wolf dog), . .	58
Bickerton, Mrs, . .	90
Bide-the-Bent, Rev. Mr, .	71
Biederman, Arnold, .	31
Biederman, Ernest, . .	31
Biederman, Rudiger, .	31
Biederman, Sigismund, .	31
Bindloose, Master, . .	121
Binks, Lady, . . .	121
Binks, Sir Bingo, . .	121
Birrenswork, Mr Herries of, ...	98
Blandeville, Lady Emily, .	94
Blattergowl, Miss Rebecca,	117
Blattergowl, Rev. Doctor,	117
Blekensop, Lady, . .	71
Bletson, Joshua, . .	58
Blok, Nikkel, . . .	27

	PAGE
Blondel (a minstrel), .	9
Blood, Colonel, . .	62
Blower, Mrs Margaret, .	121
Bohemond, of Antioch, .	1
Bois Gilbert, Sir Brian de,	14
Bolton, Captain Stawarth,	35
Boniface, Lord Abbot, .	35
Bonnyrigg, Miss Rachel, .	121
Bonsteteen, Nicholas, .	31
Bonthron, Anthony, .	22
Bothwell, Lady, . .	80
Bothwell, Sergeant, . .	67
Bouillon, Godfrey de, .	1
Bourbon, Louis, Bishop of Liège, ...	27
Bracy, Maurice de, . .	14
Bradwardine, Cosmo Comyne, . . .	94
Bradwardine, Rose, . .	94
Brenda Troil, . . .	75
Brengwan (wife of Gwenwyn), ...	5
Brenhilda, Countess of Paris, ...	1
Brennius, Nicephorus, .	1
Bridgenorth, Alice, . .	62
Bridgenorth, Major, .	62
Brittson, Sergeant, . .	35
Brown (a smuggler), .	103
Brown, Vanbeest, . .	103
Browne, General, . .	113
Buckingham, Stephen, Duke of, . . .	50
Buckingham, Villiers, Duke of, ...	62
Bucklaw, Laird of, . .	71
Bulmer, Valentine, . .	121
Bunce, John, . . .	75
Buonaventure, Father, .	98
Burgundy, Duke Charles of, ... 27,	31
Burleigh, Lord, . .	43
Butler, Reuben, . .	90
CADWALLON (a bard), .	5
Calista of Mountfauçon, Lady, ...	5
Callum Beg (a page), .	94
Cameron, Allan Break, .	107

PAGE

Campbell, General, . . 98
Campbell, Hamish, . . 86
Campbell, Helen Mac-
Gregor, . . . 86
Campbell, Robert, . . 86
Campbell, Rob Roy Mac-
Gregor, . . . 86
Campbell, Sir Duncan, . 54
Campo Basso, Count, . 31
Cargill, Rev. Josiah, . 121
Caroline, Queen of George
II., ... 90
Castor, Stephanos, . . 1
Catharine of Perth, . . 22
Catherine Seyton, . . 39
Cathleen (a servant), . 94
Caxon (a barber), . . 117
Caxon, Jenny, . . 117
Cedric, the Saxon, . . 14
Charles II., . . 58, 62
Charles, Prince of Wales, 50
Charles the Bold, of Bur-
gundy, . . . 27, 31
Charles Edward, the
Young Pretender, 94, 98
Charteris, Sir Patrick, . 22
Chattanach, MacGillie, . 22
Chatterly, Rev. Simon, . 121
Chiffinch, Mistress, . . 62
Chiffinch, William, . . 62
Christian, Edward, . . 62
Christie, Dame Nelly, . 50
Christie, John, . . 50
Christie of the Clinthill, . 35
Clara Mowbray, . . 121
Claverhouse, Colonel Gra-
ham of, . . . 67
Clement, Father, . . 22
Cleveland, Clement, . 75
Colepepper, Captain, . 50
Colin, Captain Green, . 107
Comnenus, Alexius, . . 1
Conachar (an apprentice), 22
Conrade of Montserrat,
Marquis, . . . 9
Crackenthorp, Father, . 98
Craigdallie, Bailie, . . 22
Craigenfelt, Captain, . 71
Crawford, Lindsay, Earl of, 22
Crawford, Lord, . . 27

PAGE

Crévecœur, Count Philip, 27
Crévecœur, Countess, . 27
Cromwell, Oliver, . . 58
Crosbie, Mr William, . 98
Croye, Isabella, Countess
of, ... 27
Cruickshanks, Ebenezer, . 94

DAIN, Oliver le, . . 27
Dalgarno, Lady, . . 50
Dalgarno, Lord, . . 50
Dalgetty, Sir Dugald, . 54
Dalzell, General, . . 67
Damiotti, Baptista, . . 80
Dannischemend (a sor-
cerer), . . . 31
Dannischemend, Her-
mione, . . . 31
Deans, David, . . . 90
Deans, Effie, . . . 90
Deans, Jeanie, . . . 90
Debbitch, Deborah, . 62
Dennison, Jenny, . . 67
Derby, Charlotte, Coun-
tess of, . . . 62
Derby, Earl of, . . 62
Desborough, Colonel, . 58
Dhu, Evan, . . . 54
Diana Vernon, . . 86
Dick, The Devil's, . . 22
Dickie Sludge, . . 43
Dickson, Charles, . . 18
Dickson, Tom, of Hazle-
wood, . . . 18
Digges, Miss Maria, . 121
Dinmont, Dandie, . . 103
Diogenes (a negro), . . 1
Doboobie, Doctor, . . 43
Dods, Meg, . . . 121
Donnershugel, Rudolph of, 31
Donocha Dhu, . . 90
Douban (a slave), . . 1
Dougal (a turnkey), . . 86
Douglas, Archibald, Earl
of, ... 22
Douglas, George, . . 39
Douglas, Lady, . . 39
Douglas, Sir James, . . 18
Douglas, Sir William, . 39

	PAGE
Dousterswivel, Herman, .	117
Dronsdaughter, Tronda, .	75
Dryfesdale (a steward), .	39
Dumbiedykes, Laird of, .	90
Dundee, Viscount of, .	67
Dunois, Count de, . .	27
Durward Quentin, . .	27
Dutton, Mrs, . . .	90
Dwining, Henbane, .	22
EARNSCLIFF, Patrick, .	82
Eberson, Carl, . .	27
Edith Bellenden, . .	67
Effie Deans, . . .	90
Einion, Father, . .	5
El Hadji, Barak, . .	109
Elizabeth, Queen, . .	43
Elliot, Annot, . . .	82
Elliot, Dame, . . .	82
Elliot, Hobbie, . .	82
Elliot, Jean, . . .	82
Elliot, Lilias, . . .	82
Elshie, The Dwarf, . .	82
Elspeth, Widow, . .	35
Elspeth, of Craigburn-foot, ...	117
Engaddi, Theodoric of, .	9
Erickson, Sweyne, . .	75
Ermingarde, Lady of Baldringham, . . .	5
Errol, Earl of, . . .	22
Etherington, Earl of, .	121
Eustace, Father, . .	35
Evandale, Lord, . .	67
Eveline Berenger, . .	5
Eveline Neville, . .	117
Everard, Colonel Markham, ...	58
Eviot (a page), . .	22
Ewart, Nanty, . .	98
FAGGOT, Nicholas, . .	98
Fairbrother, Mr, . .	90
Fairford, Alan, . .	98
Fairford, Mr Saunders, .	98
Fair Maid of Perth, .	22
Fairservice, Andrew, .	86
Falconer, Major, . .	80

	PAGE
Falconer, Mr, of Balmawhapple, . . .	94
Fea, Euphane, . .	75
Fenella (a dwarf), . .	62
Flammock, Rose, . .	5
Flammock, William, .	5
Fleecebumpkin, John, .	115
Fleming, Lady, . .	39
Fleming, Sir Malcolm, .	18
Flibbertigibbet, . .	43
Flora MacIvor, . .	94
Forester, Lady Jemima, .	80
Forester, Sir Philip, .	80
Foster (a champion), .	48
Foster, Anthony, . .	43
Foster, Janet, . .	43
Foxley, Squire, . .	98
France, Louis XI. of, .	27
France, Philip Augustus of, ...	9
Francis, Father, . .	22
Front de Bœuff, Reginald,	14
GABRIEL TOD, . .	103
Galbraith, Major, . .	86
Ganlesse, Richard, . .	62
Gardiner, Colonel, . .	94
Geddes, Joshua, . .	98
Geddes, Rachel, . .	98
Geierstein, Anne of, .	31
Geierstein, Count Albert of, ...	31
Gellatley, David, . .	94
Gellatley, Janet, . .	94
Genvil, Ralph, . .	5
Geraldin, Lord, . .	117
Gernington, Lady, . .	71
Gertrude Pavillon, . .	27
Gieslaer, Peterkin, . .	27
Gilfillan, Mr, . . .	94
Gillian, Dame, . .	5
Gillian, Raoul, . .	5
Gilsland, Sir Thomas de Vaux of, . . .	9
Glasgow, Bishop of, .	18
Glass, Mrs, . . .	90
Glenallan, Countess of, .	117
Glenallan, Earl of, . .	117
Glendinning, Edward, .	35

	PAGE
Glendinning, Halbert, .	35
Glendinning, Lady, . .	39
Glendinning, Sir Halbert,	39
Glendinning, Widow Elspeth, ...	35
Glenvarlock, Lord, . . .	50
Glorieux, Le (a jester), .	27
Glossin, Gilbert, . .	103
Gloucester, Earl of, . .	5
Gosling, Giles, . .	43
Gourlay, Ailsie, . .	71
Gow, Henry, . . .	22
Grace Armstrong, . .	82
Græme, Magdalen, . .	39
Græme, Roland, . .	39
Græme, Willie, of Westburnflat, . . .	82
Graham, Colonel, of Claverhouse, . .	67
Graham, Cornet, . .	67
Grantmesnel, Hugh de,	14
Gray, Gideon, . .	109
Gray, Jean, . . .	109
Gray, Menie, . .	109
Greenhorn & Grinderson, Messrs, . . .	117
Greenleaf, Gilbert, . .	18
Guarine, Philip, . .	5
Guenevra (a dwarf), .	9
Gurth (a swineherd), .	14
Guydill (a butler), . .	67
Gwenwyn, Prince of Powysland, . . .	5
HAGENBACH, Count Archibald von, . .	31
Hakim, El, . . .	9
Halcro, Claud, . .	75
Hall, Sir Christopher, .	54
Halliday, Tam, . .	67
Hameline, Lady, . .	27
Hamilton, Lady Emily,	67
Harbothel, Fabian, . .	18
Happer (a miller), . .	35
Happer, Mysie, . .	35
Harpax (a centurion), .	1
Harrison, General, . .	58
Hartley, Adam, . .	109
Hatteraick, Dirk, . .	103
	PAGE
Hautville, Lady Margaret de, ...	18
Hayraddin Mangrabin, .	27
Hayston, Frank, . .	71
Hazlewood, Charles, .	103
Headrigg, Cuddie, . .	67
Headrigg, Mause, . .	67
Helen MacGregor Campbell, ...	86
Henderson, Rev. Elias, .	39
Henry II., . . .	5
Henshaw, Kit, . .	22
Hereward (a Saxon), .	1
Heriot, George, . .	50
Hermione Dannischemend,	31
Hermione, Lady, . .	50
Herries, Mr, of Birrenswork, . . .	98
Heskett, Dame, . .	115
Heskett, Ralph, . .	115
Higg (a peasant), . .	14
Hildebrod (a bailiff), .	50
Hillary, Tom, . .	109
Hobbler, Doctor, . .	82
Hodges, John, . . .	94
Holdenough, Rev. Nehemiah, ...	58
Holiday, Master Erasmus,	43
Houghton, Humphrey, .	94
Hudson, Sir Geoffrey, .	62
Hundwolf (a steward), .	5
Hunsdon, Lord, . .	43
Huntinglen, Lord, . .	50
Hyder Ali, . . .	109
ILDERIM SHEERKOHF, .	9
Ilderton, Lucy, . .	82
Inglewood, Squire, . .	86
Ireby, Mr, . . .	115
Irene, The Empress, .	1
Irwin, Hannah, . .	121
Isaac of York, . . .	14
Isabel Vere, . . .	82
Isabella Wardour, . .	117
Ivanhoe, Wilfrid of, . .	14
JACQUELINE (a servant), .	27
James I., . . .	50

	PAGE
Janet of Tomahourich,	115
Jarvie, Bailie Nicol, .	86
Jekyl, Captain,	121
Jerningham (a secretary), .	62
Jerome, Abbot,	18
Joan, Princess of France, .	27
Jobson, Joseph,	86
John, Prince, brother of Richard I., .	14
John, Prince, son of Henry II., .	5
Joliffe, Jocelin,	58
Jorworth ap Jevan, .	5
Jourvaulx, Abbot of,	14
Julia Mannering,	103
KENNEDY, Frank, .	103
Kenneth, Sir, of the Couchant Leopard,	9
Kerneguy, Louis, .	58
Kettledrumle, Gabriel,	67
Knock, Duncan,	90
LACY, Damian,	5
Lacy, Ranald, .	5
Lacy, Sir Hugo de, .	5
Lambourne, Michael,	43
Langley, Sir Frederick,	82
Latimer, Darsie,	98
Lauderdale, Duke of,	67
Lawford, Mr, .	109
Lee, Albert, .	58
Lee, Alice, .	58
Lee, Sir Henry,	58
Leicester Dudley, Earl of,	43
Leopold, Archduke of Austria,	9
Lesley, Ludovic, le Balafré,	27
Liège, Louis Bourbon, Bishop of, .	27
Lilias Redgauntlet, .	98
Lindesay, Lord,	39
Linklater, Lawrence,	50
Littlejohn, Bailie, .	117
Lochleven, Lady of,	39
Locksley (an outlaw),	14
Louis XI. of France,	27
Louise (a minstrel), .	22

	PAGE
Lovell, Mr William,	117
Lowestoffe, Reginald,	50
Lucy Ashton, .	71
Lunden, Sir Louis, .	22
Lyle, Annot, .	54
Lysimachus (a designer), .	1
MACALPINE, Jean, .	86
MacAulay, Allan	54
MacAulay, Angus, .	54
MacBriar (a preacher),	67
MacCallum More, Duke of Argyle, .	90
MacCallum More, Marquis of Argyle, .	54
MacCandlish, Mrs, .	103
MacClure, Bessie, .	67
MacCombich, Evan Dhu, .	94
MacCombich, Robin Oig.	115
MacEagh, Kenneth,	54
MacEagh, Ranald, .	54
MacFittoch, Mr, .	109
MacGuffog (a constable), .	103
MacIan, Eachin,	22
MacIlduy (a chieftain), .	54
MacIntyre, Captain Hector,	117
MacIntyre, Miss Maria, .	117
MacIvor, Fergus, Vich Ian Vohr, .	94
MacIvor, Flora, .	94
MacLeuchar, Mrs, .	117
MacMorlan, Mr and Mrs,	103
MacStuart (a trooper),	86
MacTurk, Captain Hector,	121
MacVittie and MacFin, Messrs,	86
MacWheeble, Bailie,	94
Madge Wildfire,	90
Mahony, Dugald,	94
Mailsetter, Mrs,	117
Malagrowther, Sir Mungo,	50
Malvoisin, Conrade de,	14
Malvoisin, Richard de,	14
Malvoisin, Sir Philip de,	14
Mangrabin, Hayraddin,	27
Mannering, Colonel Guy, .	103
Mannering, Julia, .	103
Mannering, Mrs,	103
Mansell, Lady,	50

	PAGE
Marabout (a fanatic),	9
March, Earl of,	22
Marck, William de la,	27
Mareschal, Ralph,	82
Margaret of Anjou,	31
Margaret Ramsay,	50
Martha (a servant),	86
Martha Trapbois,	50
Marthon (a gipsy woman),	27
Mary Avenel,	35
Mary, Queen of Scots,	39
Mattie (a servant),	86
Mauley, Sir Edward,	82
Maulstatute, Master,	62
Maxwell (an usher),	50
Maxwell, Mr Peter,	98
Mayflower, Phœbe,	58
Meg Dods,	121
Meg Merrilies,	103
Meg Murdockson,	90
Meikleham, Mr Saunders,	121
Melville, Major,	94
Melville, Sir Robert,	39
Mengs, Jan,	31
Menie Gray,	109
Menteith, Earl of,	54
Meredith, Mr Michael,	121
Merrilies, Meg,	103
Mertoun, Mr Basil,	75
Mertoun, Mordaunt,	75
Mervyn, Mr and Mrs,	103
Minna Troil,	75
Mist, Children of the,	54
Moffat, Mabel,	98
Mohr, Elspet,	107
Mohr, Hamish Bean,	107
Mohr, Hamish MacTavish,	107
Monçada, Mddle. Zilia de,	109
Monçada, Mathias de,	109
Monçada, Richard,	109
Monkbarns, Mr Oldbuck of,	117
Monmouth, Duke of,	67
Monna Paula,	50
Monoplies, Richie,	50
Monthermer, Sir Guy,	5
Montreville, Madame de,	109
Montrose, Earl of,	54
Montserrat, Conrade, Marquis of,	9

	PAGE
Morolt, Dennis,	5
Morrison, Hugh, of Glanae,	115
Morton, Henry,	67
Morton, Lord,	35
Morton, Mr,	67
Morton, Rev. Mr,	94
Mountfauçon, Lady Calista of,	9
Mowbray, Clara,	121
Mowbray, John,	121
Muckiebackit, Saunders,	117
Mucklewraith (a fanatic),	67
Mulgrave, Sir Miles,	54
Multon, Sir Thomas de,	9
Mumps, Tib,	103
Murdockson, Meg,	90
Murray, Earl of,	35, 39
Mysie Happer,	35
Necbatanus (a dwarf),	9
Neville, Eveline,	117
Neville, Major,	117
Nicanor (a Greek),	1
Nixon, Cristal,	98
Norna of the Fitful Head,	75
Ochiltree, Edie,	117
Oldbuck, Miss Griselda,	117
Oldbuck, Mr Jonathan, of Monkbarns,	117
Olifant, Basil,	67
Olifaunt, Nigel,	50
Oliver Cromwell,	58
Orleans, Duke Louis of,	27
Ormond, Duke of,	62
Osbaldistone, Frank,	86
Osbaldistone, Mr William,	86
Osbaldistone, Rashleigh,	86
Osbaldistone, Sir Hildebrand,	86
Otranto, Prince Tancred of,	1
Outram, Lance,	62
Oxford, Earl of,	31
Owen, Mr,	86
Pacolet, Nicholas,	75

	PAGE
Paris, Brenhilda, Countess of,	1
Paris, Count Robert of,	1
Pate in Peril,	98
Paula, Monna,	50
Paupiah (a steward),	109
Pavillon (a currier),	27
Pearson, Captain,	58
Peebles, Peter,	98
Pembroke, Earl of,	18
Pembroke, Mr,	94
Penfeather, Lady Penelope,	121
Perrette, Dame,	27
Peter, the Hermit,	1
Peveril, Julian,	62
Peveril, Lady Margaret,	62
Peveril, Sir Geoffrey,	62
Phadraick, Miles,	107
Philip, Father,	35
Philip Augustus, of France,	9
Philpson, John,	31
Pierre, Maitre,	27
Plantagenet, Lady Edith,	9
Pleydell, Mr Paulus,	103
Polwarth, Alick,	94
Porteous, Captain,	90
Poundtext (a preacher),	67
Powheid, Lazarus,	18
Pretender, The Young,	94, 98
Proudfute, Oliver,	22
QUACKLEBEN, Doctor Quentin,	121
Quentin Durward,	27
RALEIGH, Sir Walter,	43
Ramorny, Sir John,	22
Ramsay, David,	50
Ramsay, Margaret,	50
Randal (a boatman),	39
Ratcliffe, Jim,	90
Ratcliffe, Mr Hubert,	82
Ravenswood, Edgar,	71
Raymond, Count of Toulouse,	1
Rebecca of York,	14
Redgauntlet, Laird of,	98
Redgauntlet, Lilias,	98

	PAGE
Redgauntlet, Sir Arthur Darsie,	98
Reinold (a butler),	5
René, King of Provence,	31
Richard I.,	9, 14
Richard, Prince, son of Henry II.,	5
Robert, Count of Paris,	1
Robert III., of Scotland,	22
Robertson, George,	90
Robin Hood,	14
Rob Roy MacGregor Campbell,	86
Robsart, Amy,	43
Robsart, Sir Hugh,	43
Rochecliffe, Doctor Anthony,	58
Ronaldson, Neil,	75
Rose Bradwardine,	94
Rose Flammock,	5
Rothsay, David, Duke of,	22
Rowena, Lady,	14
Rudolph of Donnershugel,	31
Ruthven (a pedlar),	94
Ruthven, Lord,	39
SADDLETREE, Mr Bartolini,	90
St Ronan's, Laird of,	121
Saladin, Sultan,	9
Sampson, Dominie,	103
Scambester, Eric,	75
Schreechwald, Ital,	31
Scotland, Prince Royal of,	9
Scots, Mary Queen of,	39
Scrogie, Mr Peregrine Touchwood,	121
Scrow (a clerk),	103
Sebastes (a recruit),	1
Seelencooper, Captain,	109
Seyton, Catherine,	39
Seyton, Henry,	39
Seyton, Lord,	39
Shafton, Sir Piercie,	35
Sharpitlaw (a constable),	90
Sheerkohf, Ilderim,	9
Simon (a glover),	22
Skurliewhitter, Andrew,	50
Sludge, Dick,	43
Smith, Wayland,	43

	PAGE
Smith, Will, . . .	62
Snailsfoot, Bryce, . .	75
Solmes (a valet), . .	121
Solsgroves, Rev. Nehemiah,	62
Spitfire (a page), . .	58
Staunton, George, . .	90
Staunton, Sir Edmund, .	90
Steenson, Willie. . .	98
Stewart, Francis, . .	67
Strauchan (a squire), .	9
Strumpfer, Nicholas, .	75
Sturmthal, Melchior, .	31
Suddlechop, Benjamin, .	50
Suddlechop, Dame Ursula,	50
Swertha (a servant), .	75
Sylvan (an ourang-outang)	1
TACKET, Martin, . .	35
Tacket, Tibb, . . .	35
Taffril, Lieutenant, . .	117
Talbot, Colonel, . .	94
Tancred, Prince of Otranto,	1
Tatius, Achilles, . .	1
Templars, Grand Master of the, ...	9, 14
Theodoric of Engadui, .	9
Thornton, Captain, . .	86
Tippoo Saib, . . .	109
Tod, Gabriel, . . .	103
Toison d'Or (a herald), .	27
Tomahourich, Janet of, .	115
Tombs, Knight of 'he, .	18
Tomkins, Joseph, . .	58
Topham, Charles, . .	62
Torquil of the Oak, . .	22
Touchwood, Mr Peregrine Scrogie, ...	121
Toulouse, Count Raymond of, . . .	1
Tower, Governor of the, .	50
Toxartis (a Scythian), .	1
Traobois (a lodging-house keeper), ...	50
Trapbois, Martha, . .	50
Tresham, Richard, . .	109
Tressilian, Master, . .	43
Tristran, l'Hermite, . .	27
Troil, Brenda, . . .	75
Troil, Magnus, . .	75

	PAGE
Troil, Minna, . . .	75
Troil, Ulla, . . .	75
Trotter, Nelly, . .	121
Trumbull, Tam, . .	98
Tuck, Friar, . . .	14
Tunstall, Francis, . .	50
Turnbull, Michael, . .	18
Tyre, Archbishop of, .	9
Tyrie, Rev. Michael, .	107
Tyrrel, Francis, . .	121
ULRICA, Dame, . .	14
Una (a servant) . .	94
Ursel, Zedekias, . .	1
Ursula, Sister, . .	18
VALENCE, Sir Aymer de,	18
Vanbeest Brown, . .	103
Varney, Richard, . .	43
Vaudemond, Ferrand de, .	31
Vaughan, Basil, . .	75
Vaughan, Clement, . .	75
Vaux, Sir Thomas de, of Gilsland, . . .	9
Vehemique, Tribunal Knights and Burghers of,	31
Veilchen, Annette, . .	31
Vere, Arthur de, . .	31
Vere, Isabel, . . .	82
Vere, Mr Richard, . .	82
Vermandois, Count de, .	1
Vernon, Diana, . .	86
Vernon, Sir Frederick, .	86
Vich Ian Vohr, Fergus MacIvor, . . .	94
Vincent, Jenkin, . .	50
Violante (an attendant), .	1
Vipont, Ralph de, . .	14
WAKEFIELD, Harry, .	115
Wales, Prince Charles of,	50
Wallenrode, Earl, . .	9
Walton, Sir John de, .	18
Wamba (a jester), . .	14
Warden, Rev. Henry,	35, 39
Wardour, Captain Reginald, ...	117

	PAGE		PAGE
Wardour, Isabella, . .	117	Witherington, Mrs . .	109
Wardour, Sir Arthur, .	117	Wittenbold, Captain, .	67
Waverley, Edward, . .	94	Woodcock, Adam, . .	39
Waverley, Miss Rachel, .	94	Woodville, Lord, . .	113
Waverley, Richard, .	94		
Waverley, Sir Everard, .	94		
Weatherport, Captain, .	75	YELLOWLEY, Barbara, .	75
Westburnflat, Willie Graeme of, . . .	82	Yellowley, Triptolemus, .	75
Wildfire, Madge, . .	90		
Wildrake, Captain Roger,	58	ZAMET (a gipsy), . .	27
Wilson, Andrew, . .	90	Zarah (a dwarf), . .	62
Wilson, Dame Alison, .	67	Zimmerman, Adam, .	31
Winterblossom, Mr Phillip,	121	Zosimus (Greek Patri-	
Witherington, General, .	109	arch)	1

THE END